Welcome to Colors of Serenity: A Coloring Book to Relax and De-stress, a unique and transformative journey that invites you to explore the pages of this coloring book as a search for serenity and tranquility.

Colors of Serenity: A Coloring Book to Relax and Destress is more than just a coloring book; It is an invitation to rediscover the beauty of every stroke, every hue. Each page is an opportunity to escape the hustle and bustle of everyday life, find inner peace, and express your creativity in a therapeutic way.

Enjoy the journey that starts now. What Colors of Serenity: A Coloring Book to Relax and De-stress will guide you to a state of calm and balance, offering precious moments of self-reflection and inner peace.

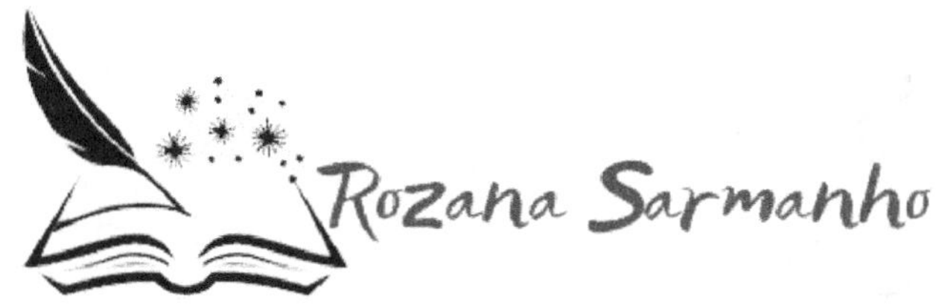

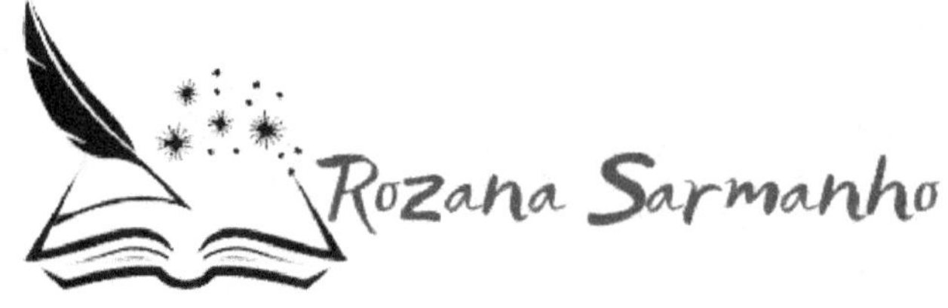

Rozana Sarmanho

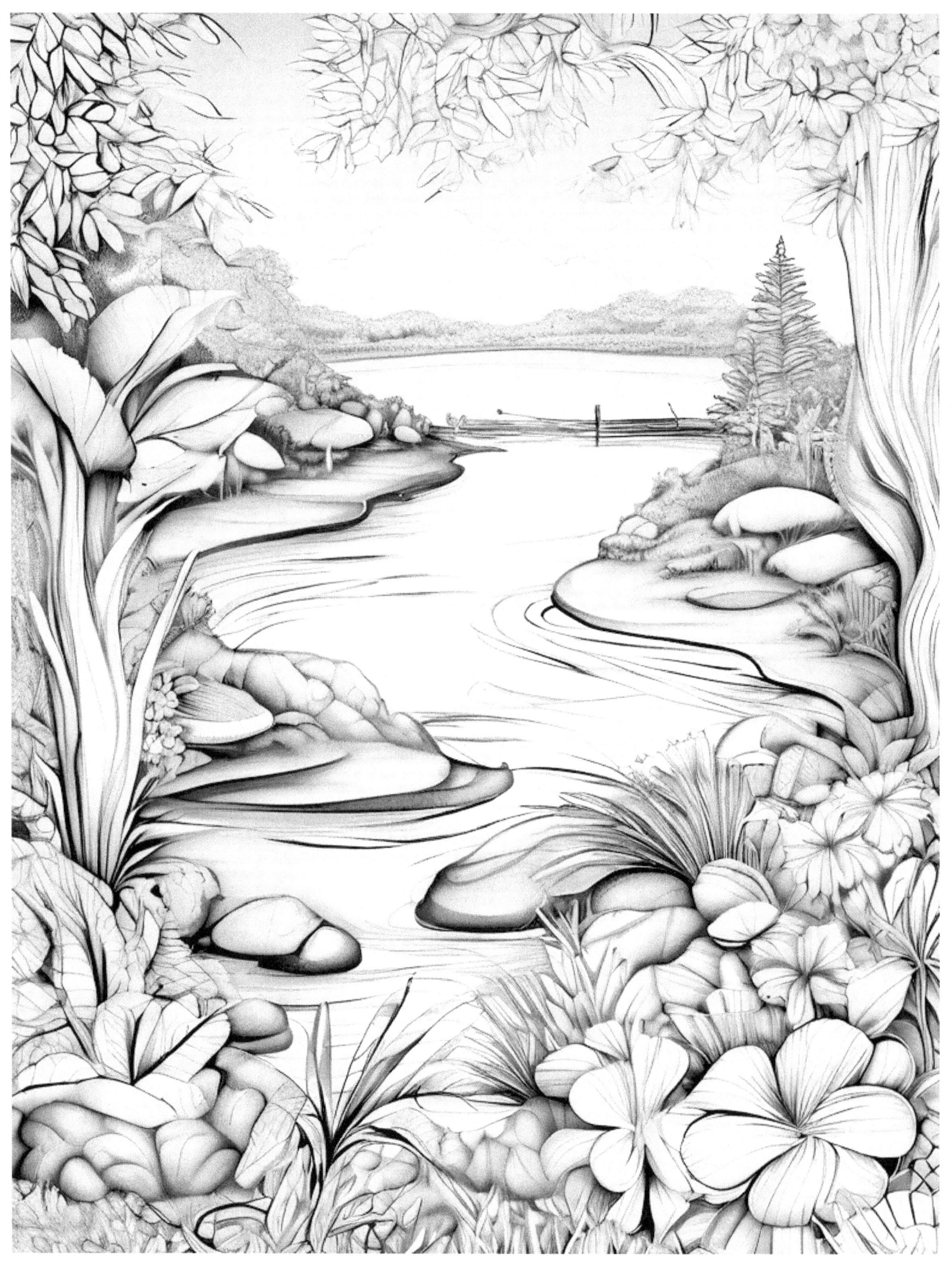

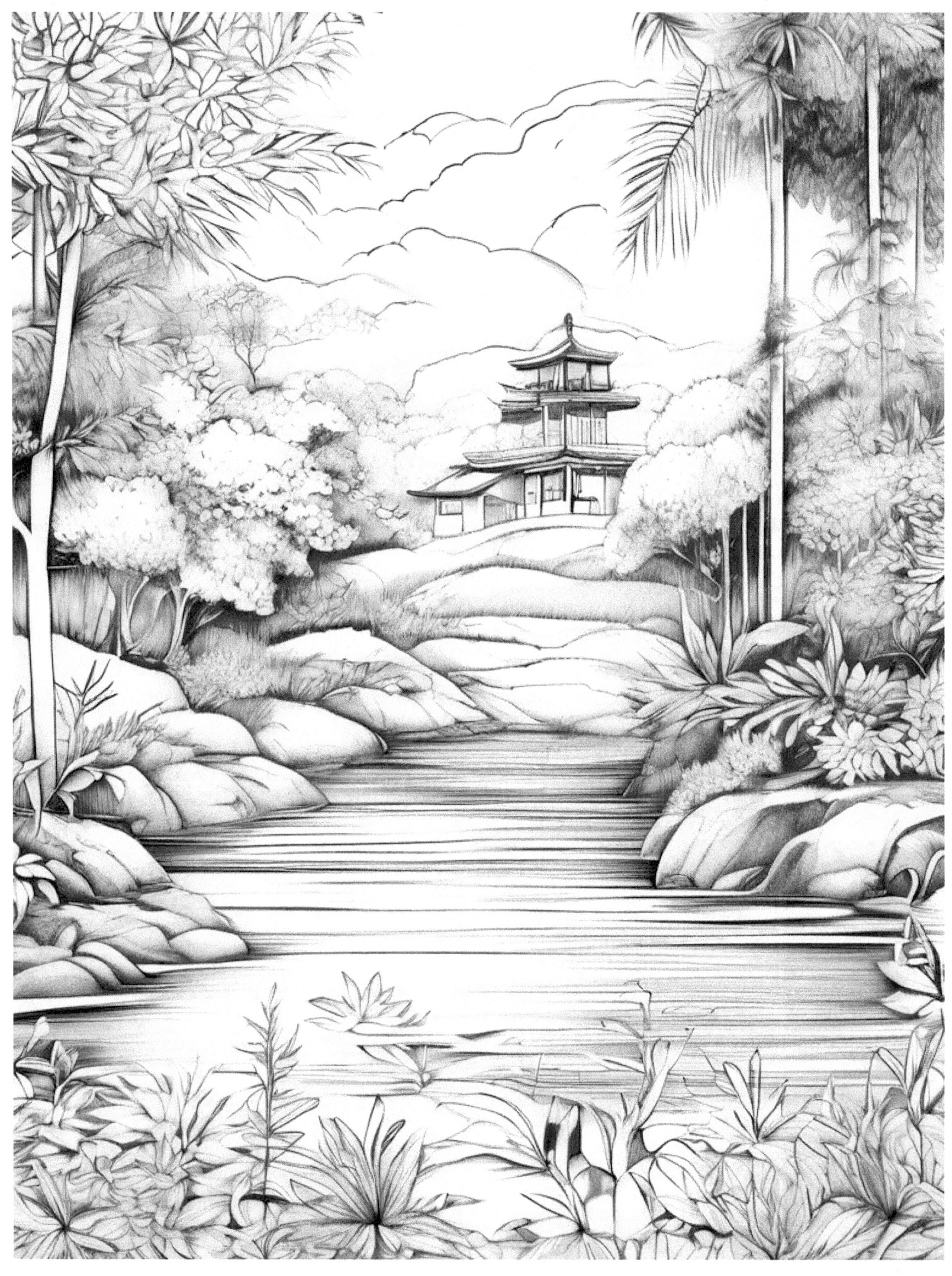

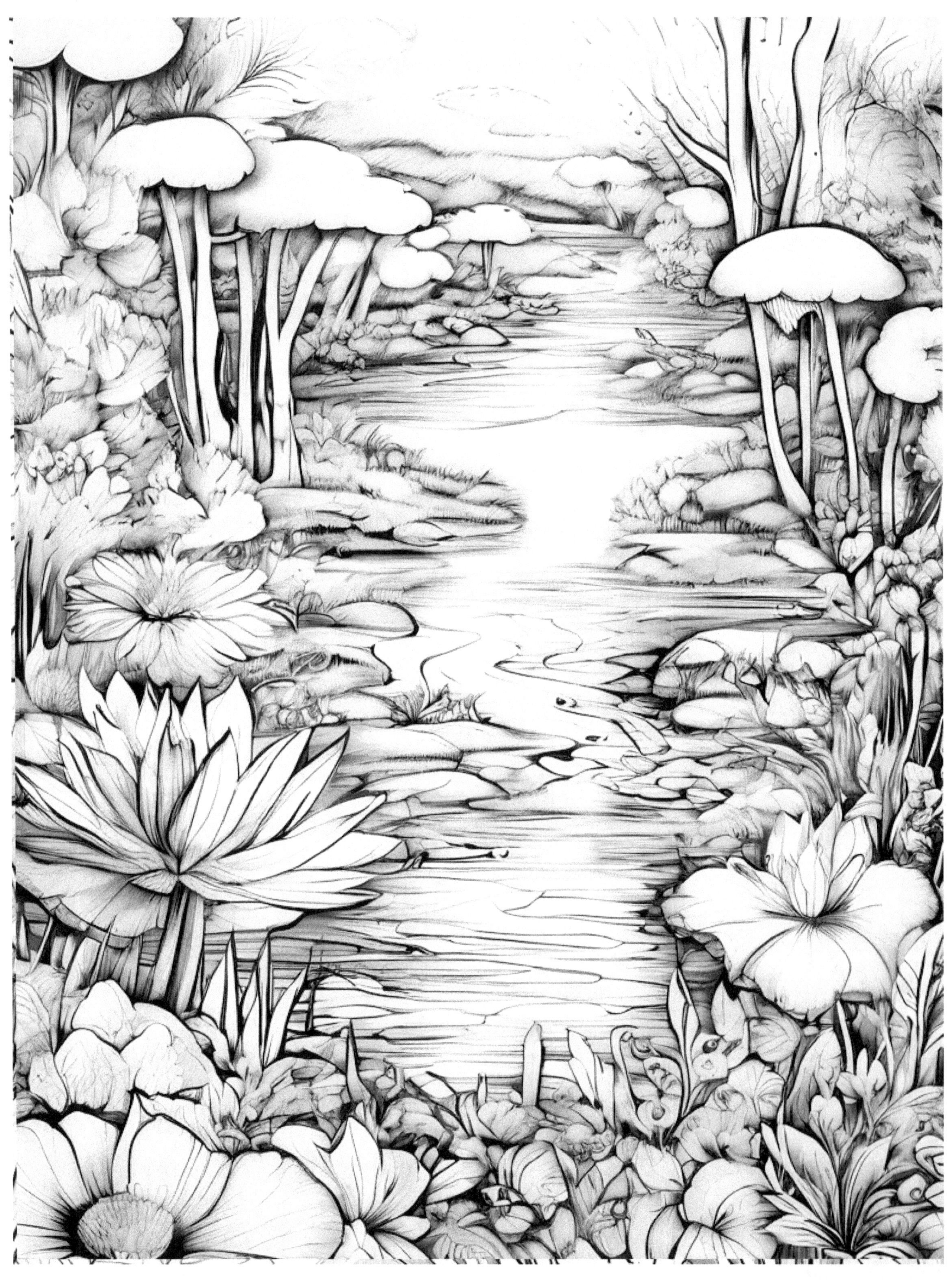

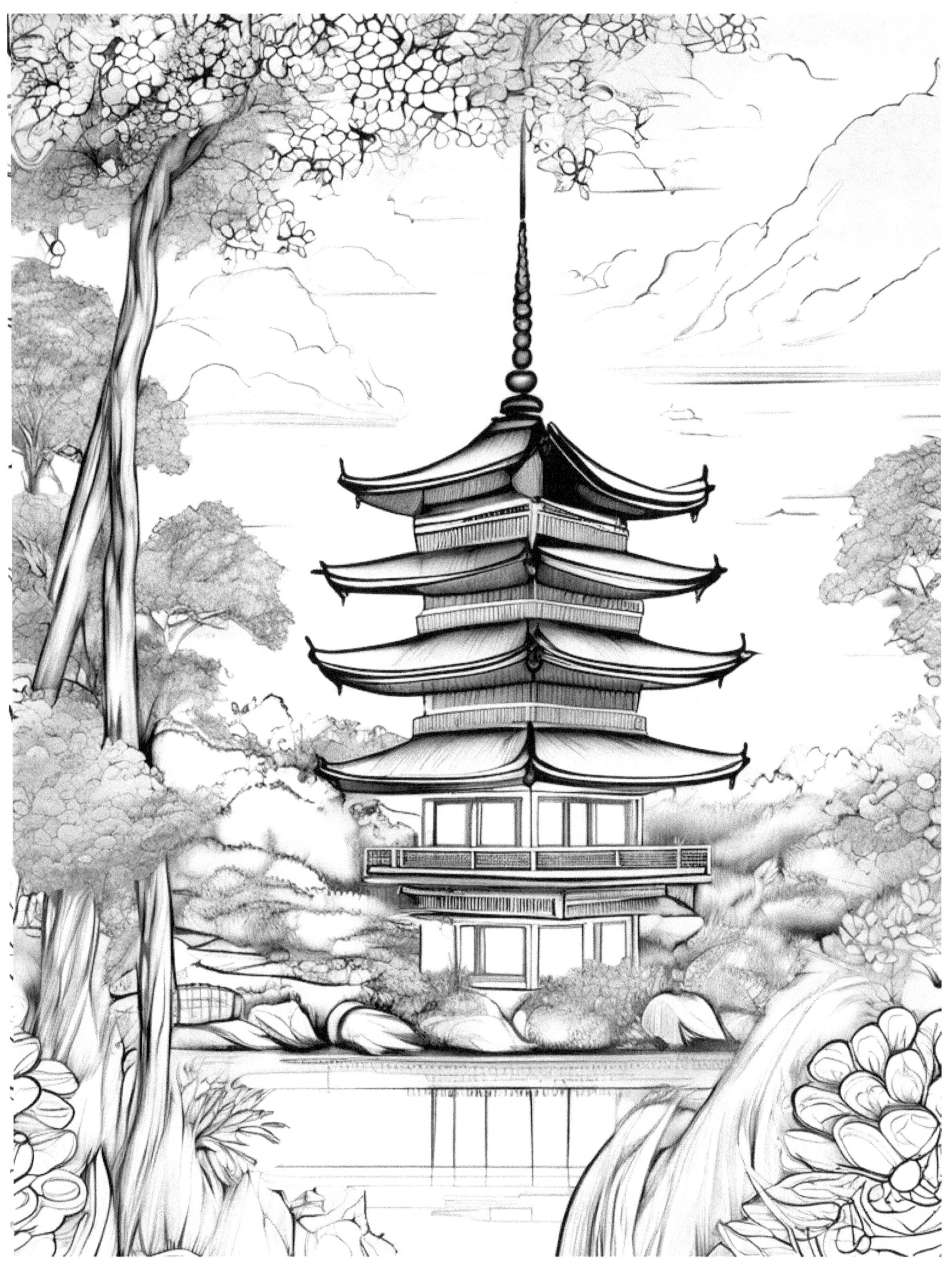

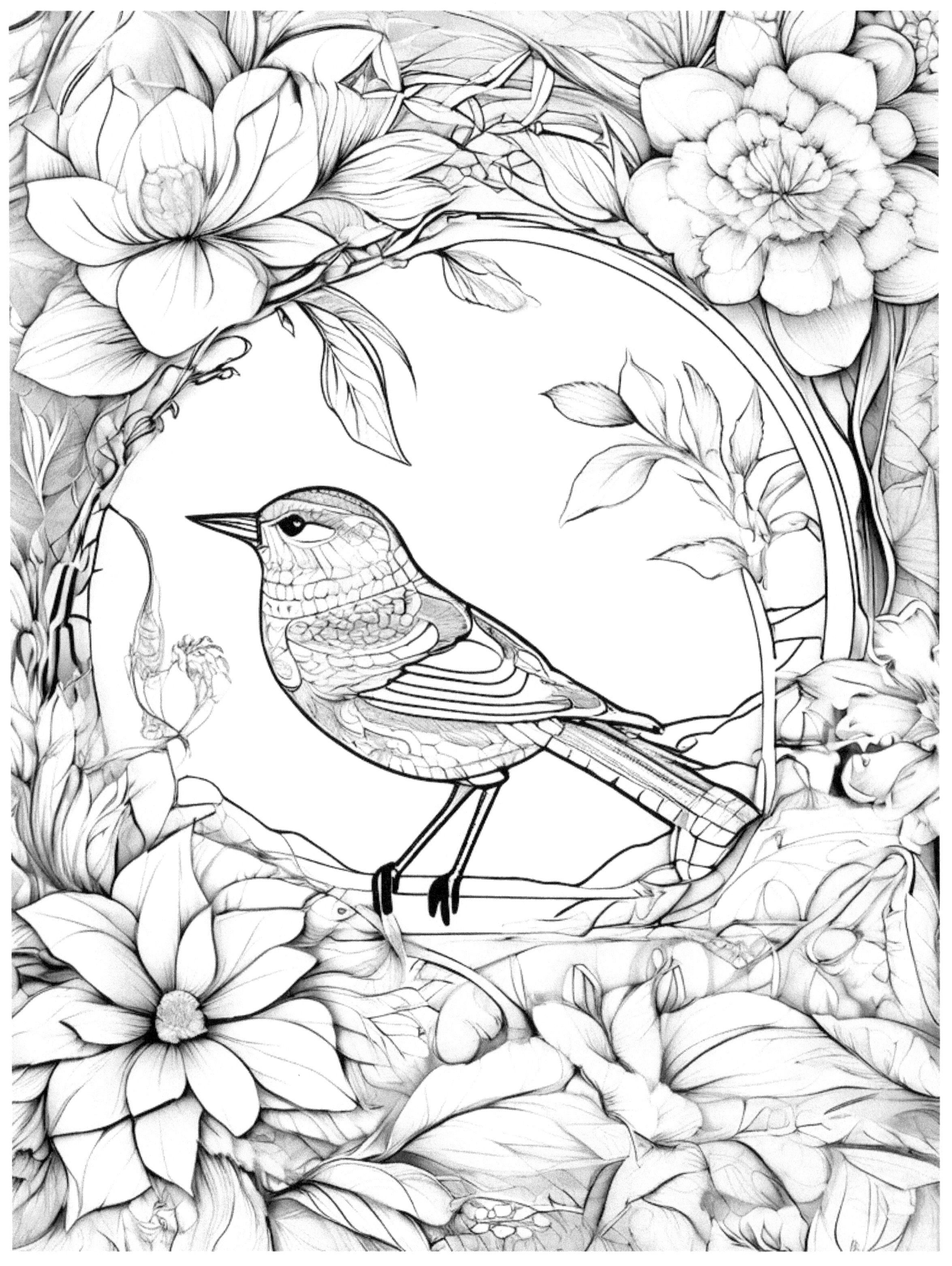

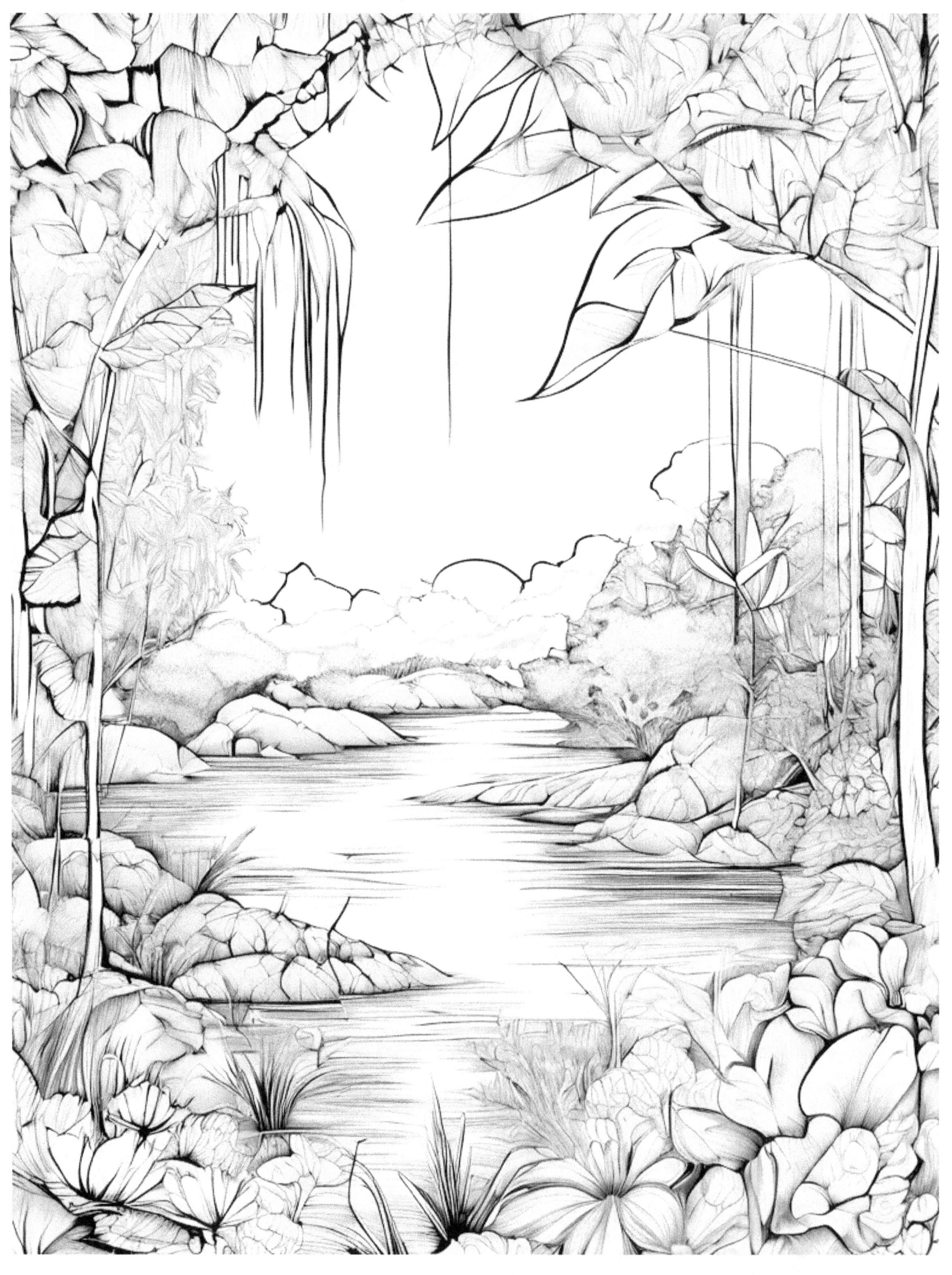

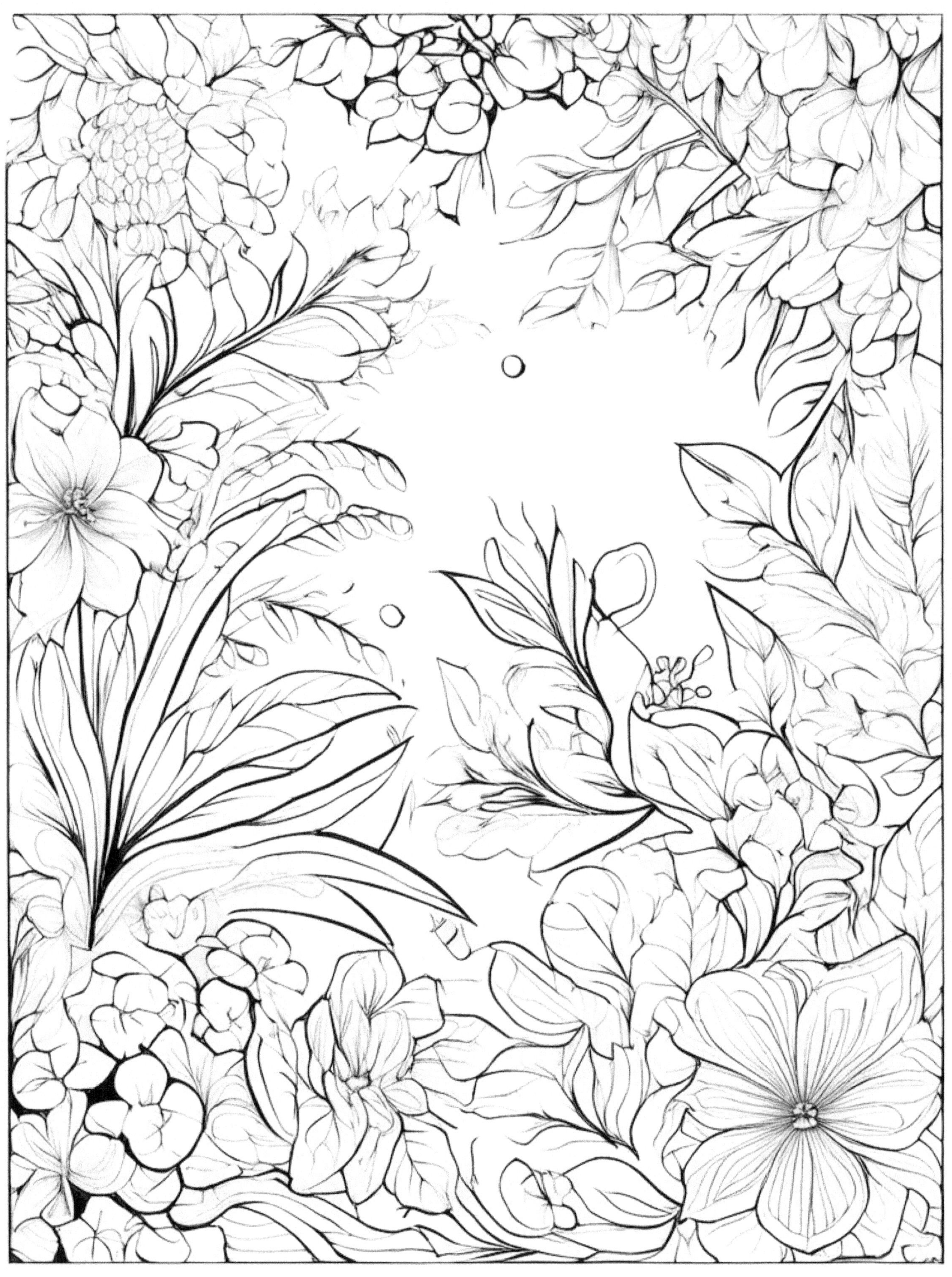

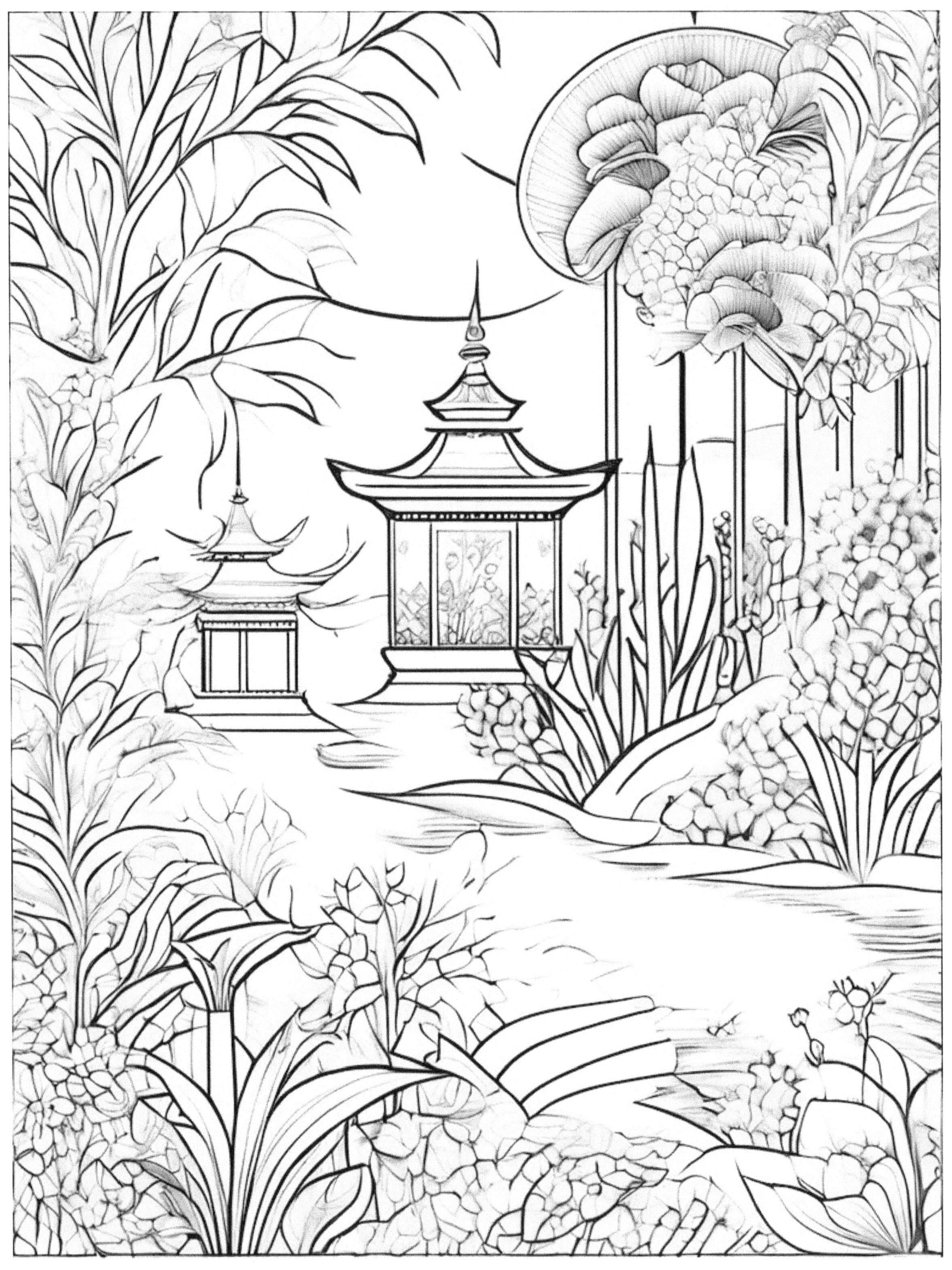

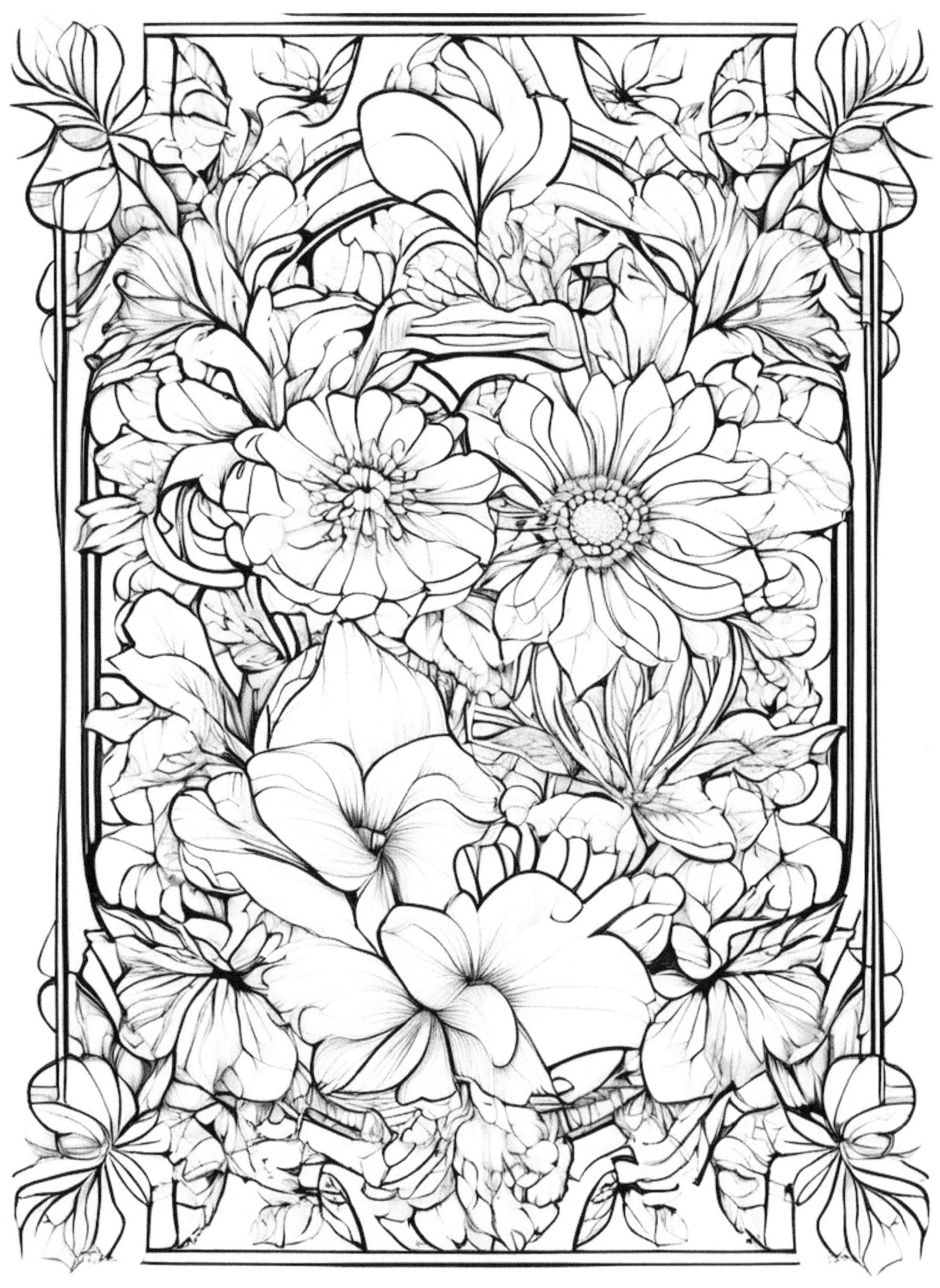

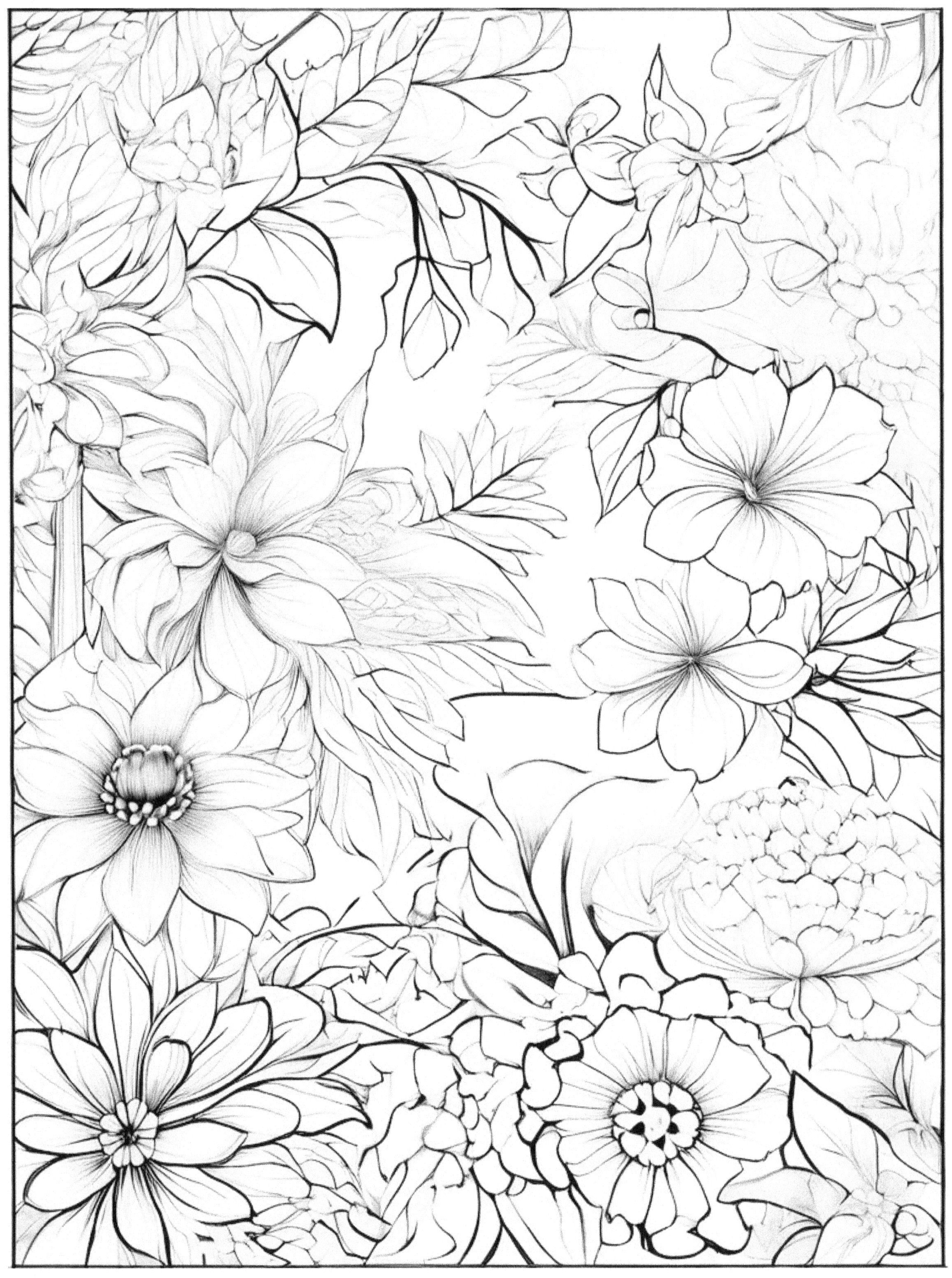

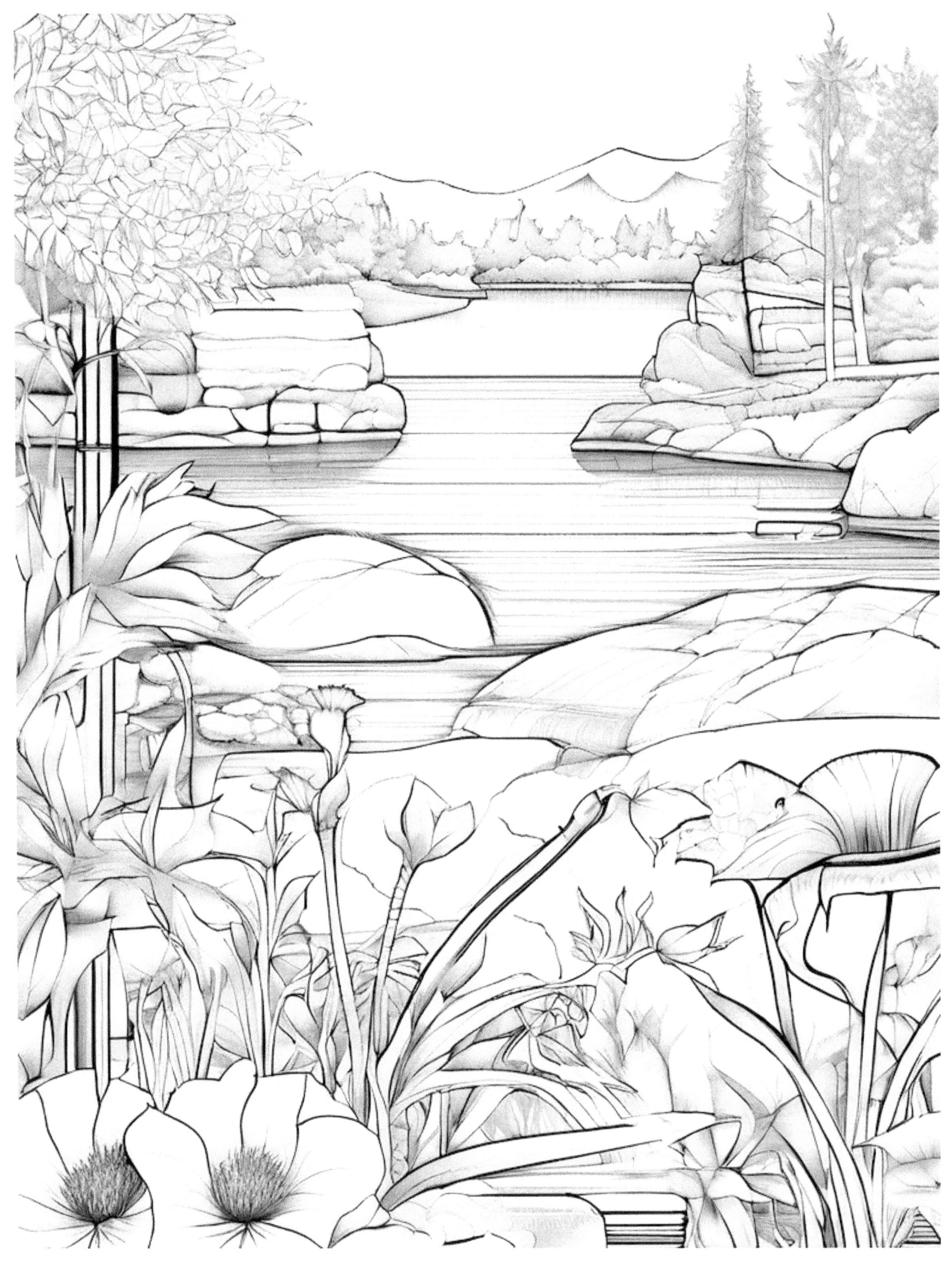

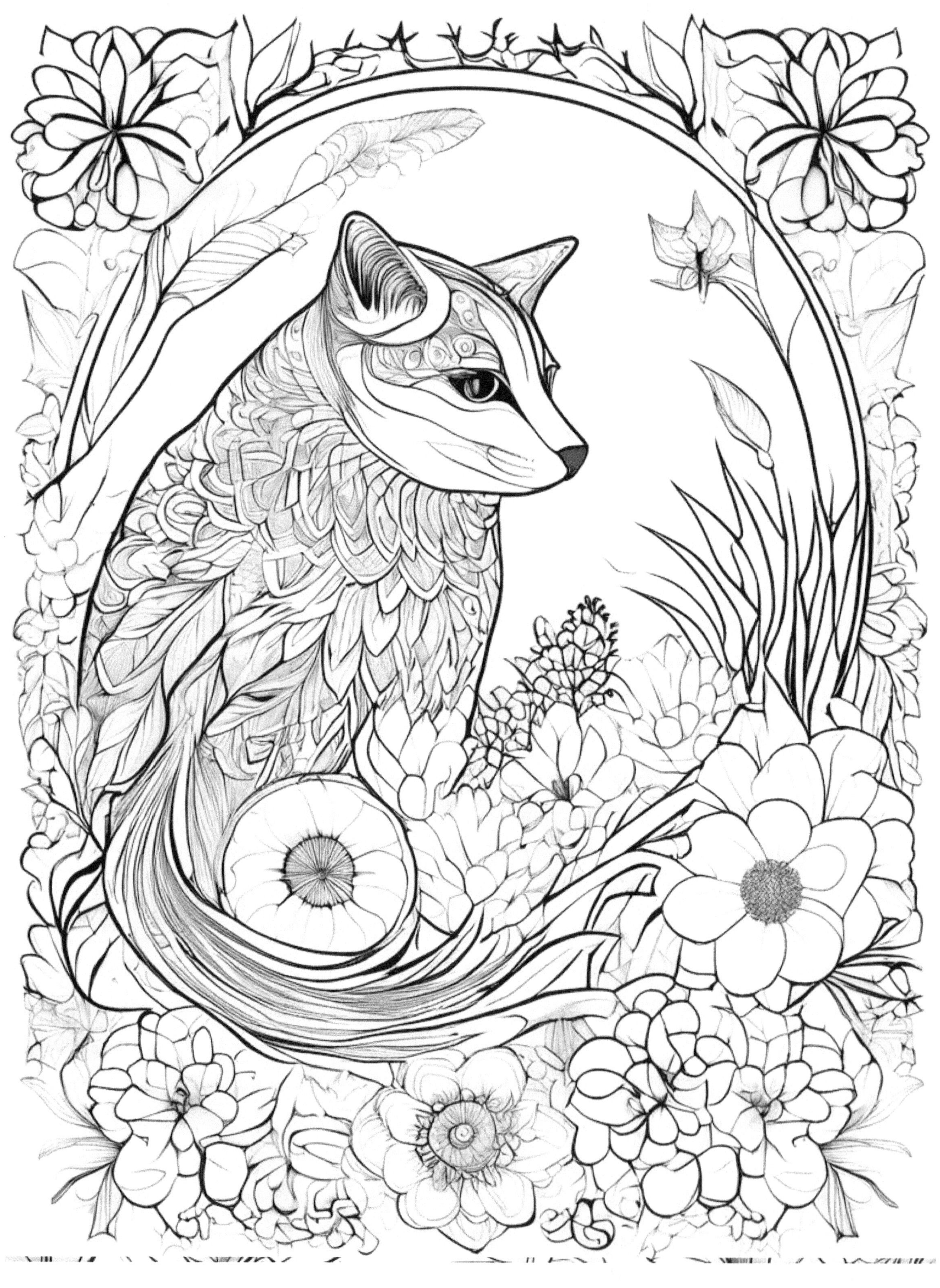

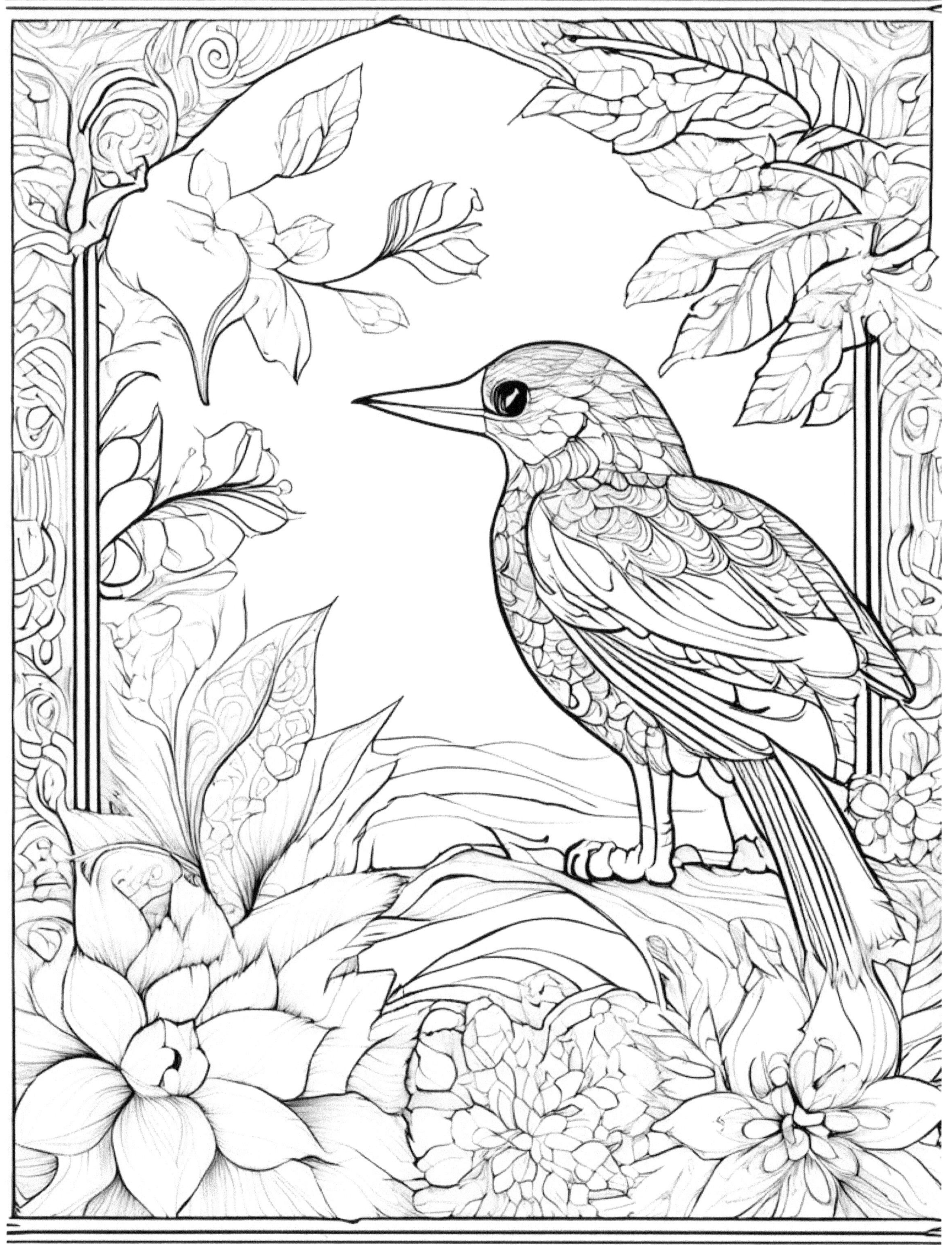

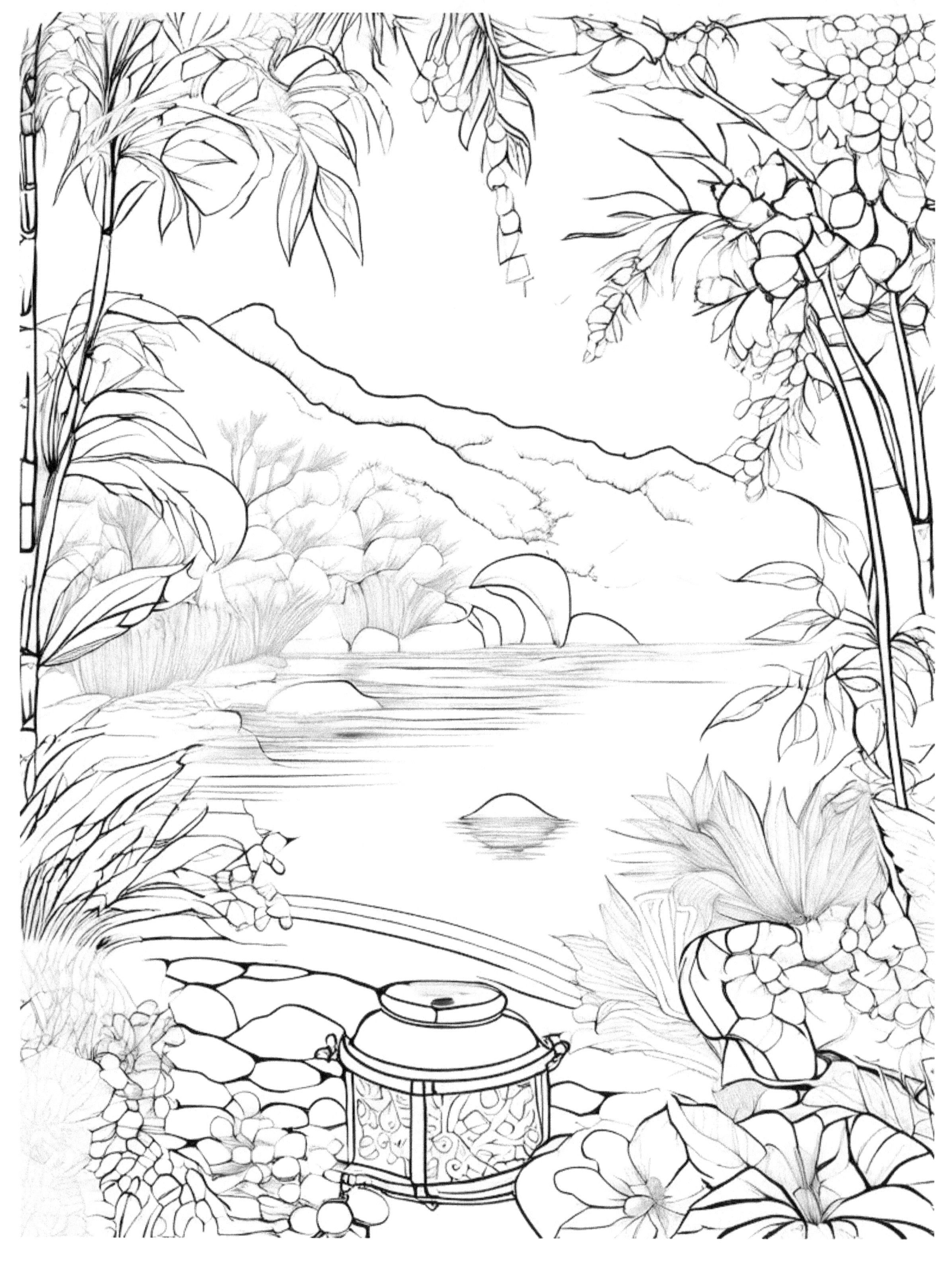

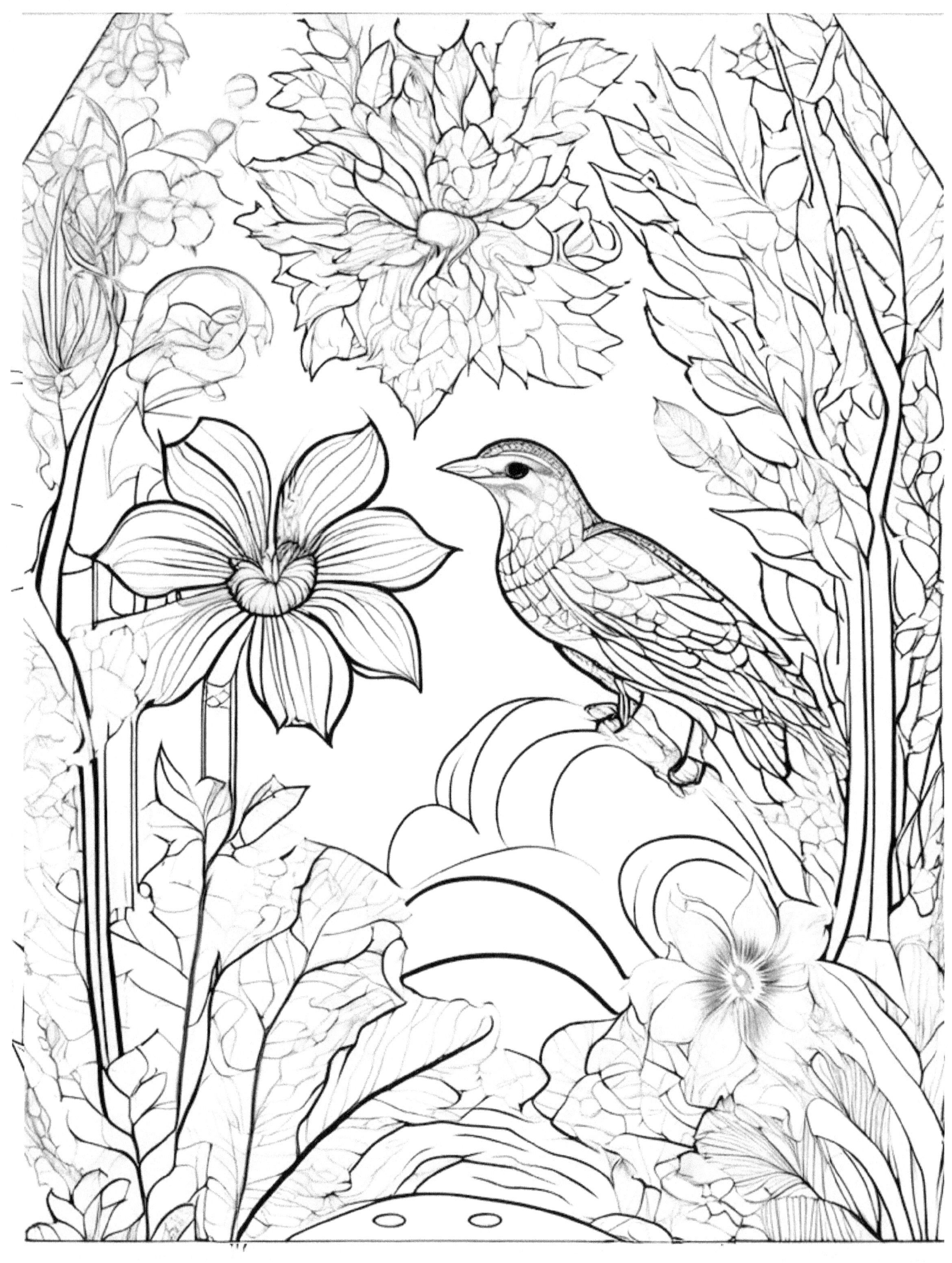

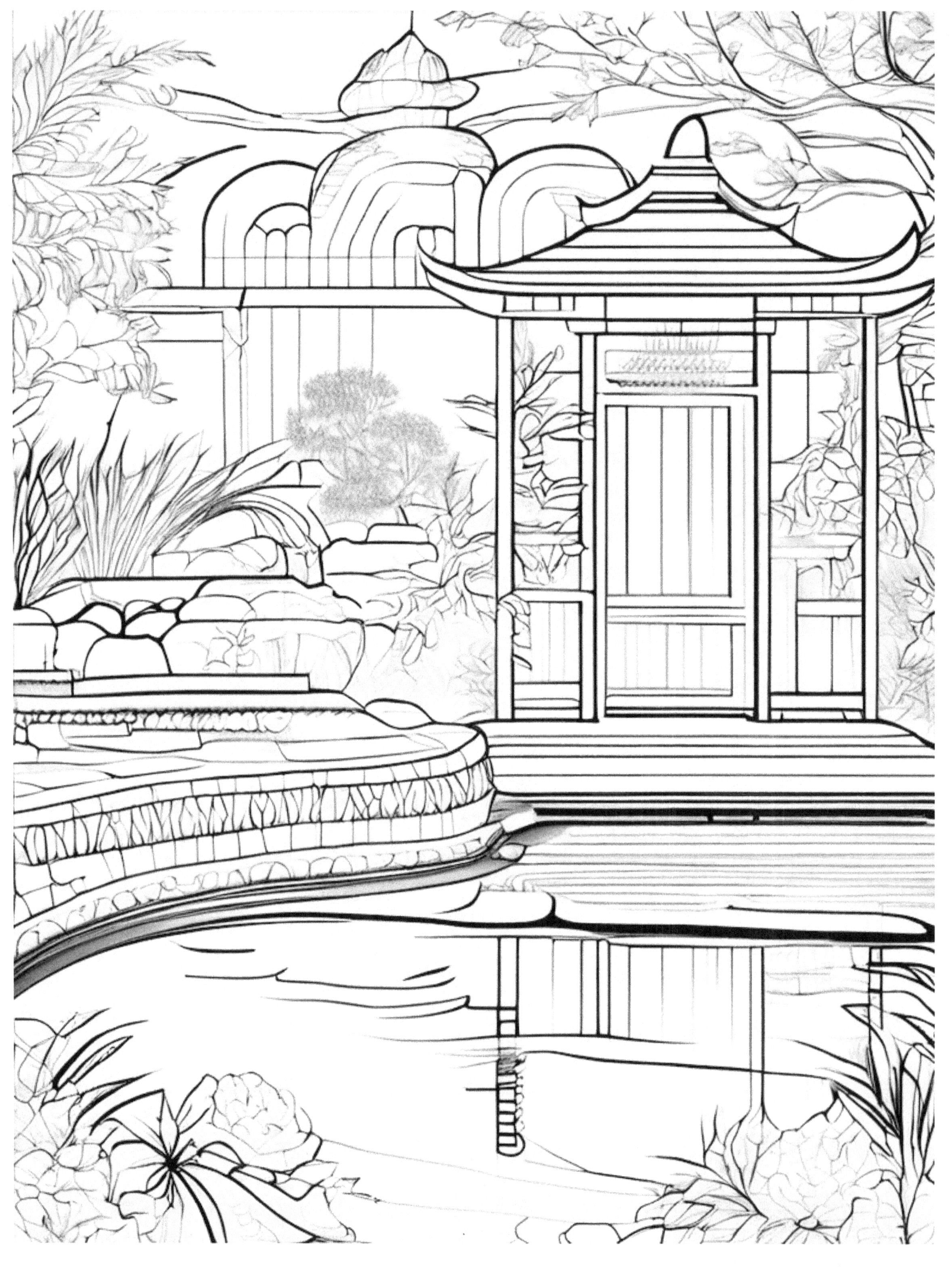

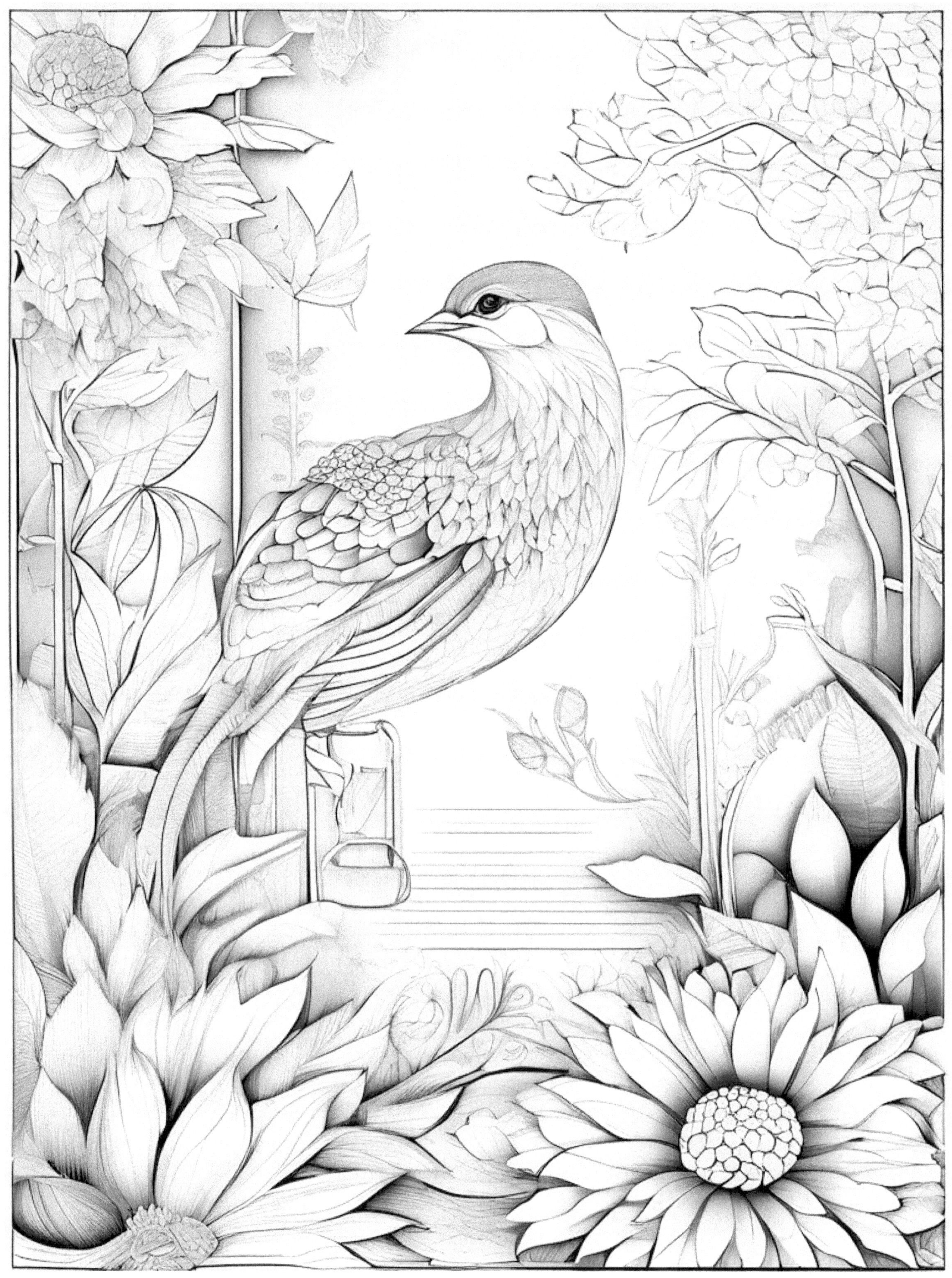

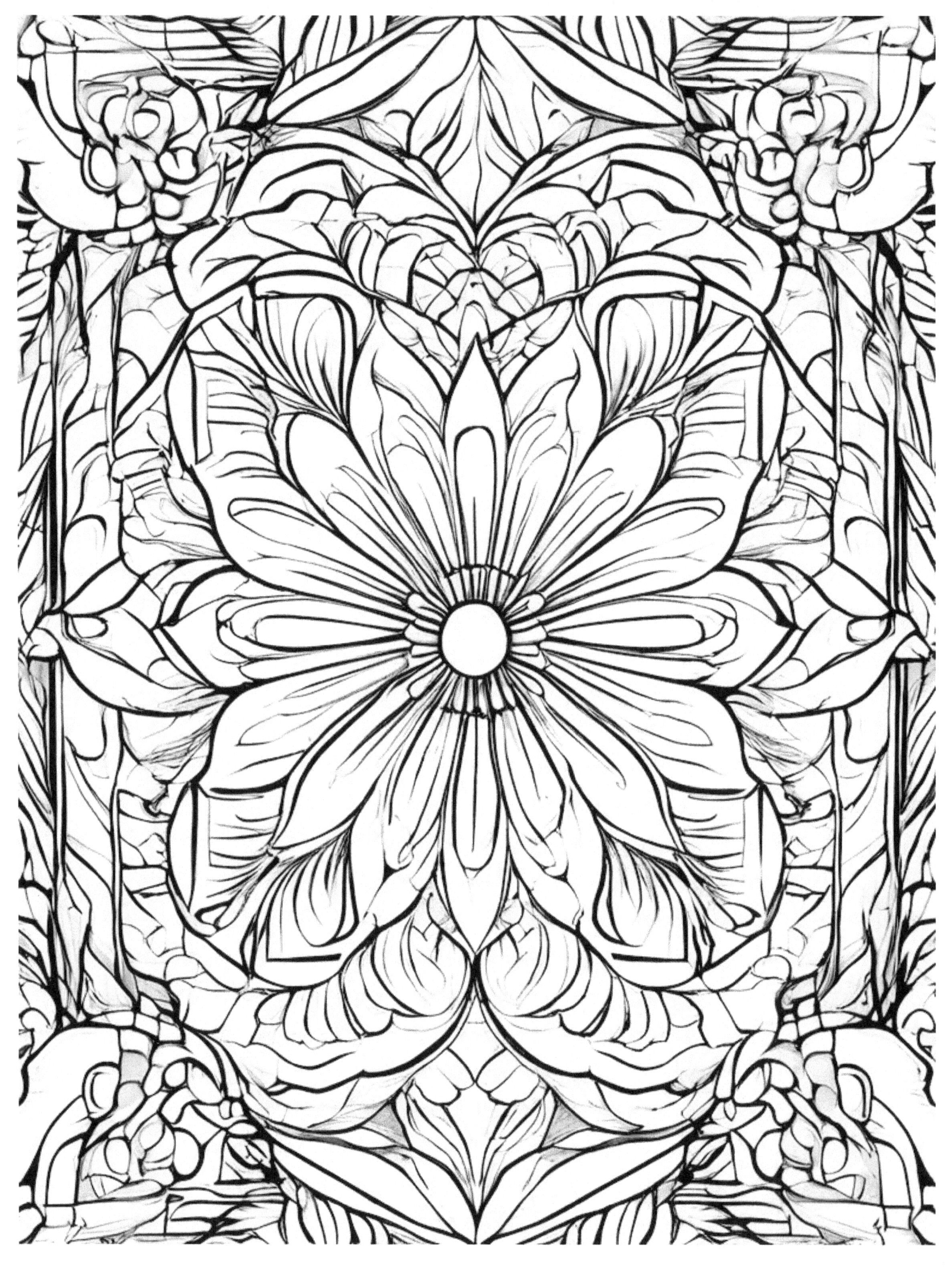

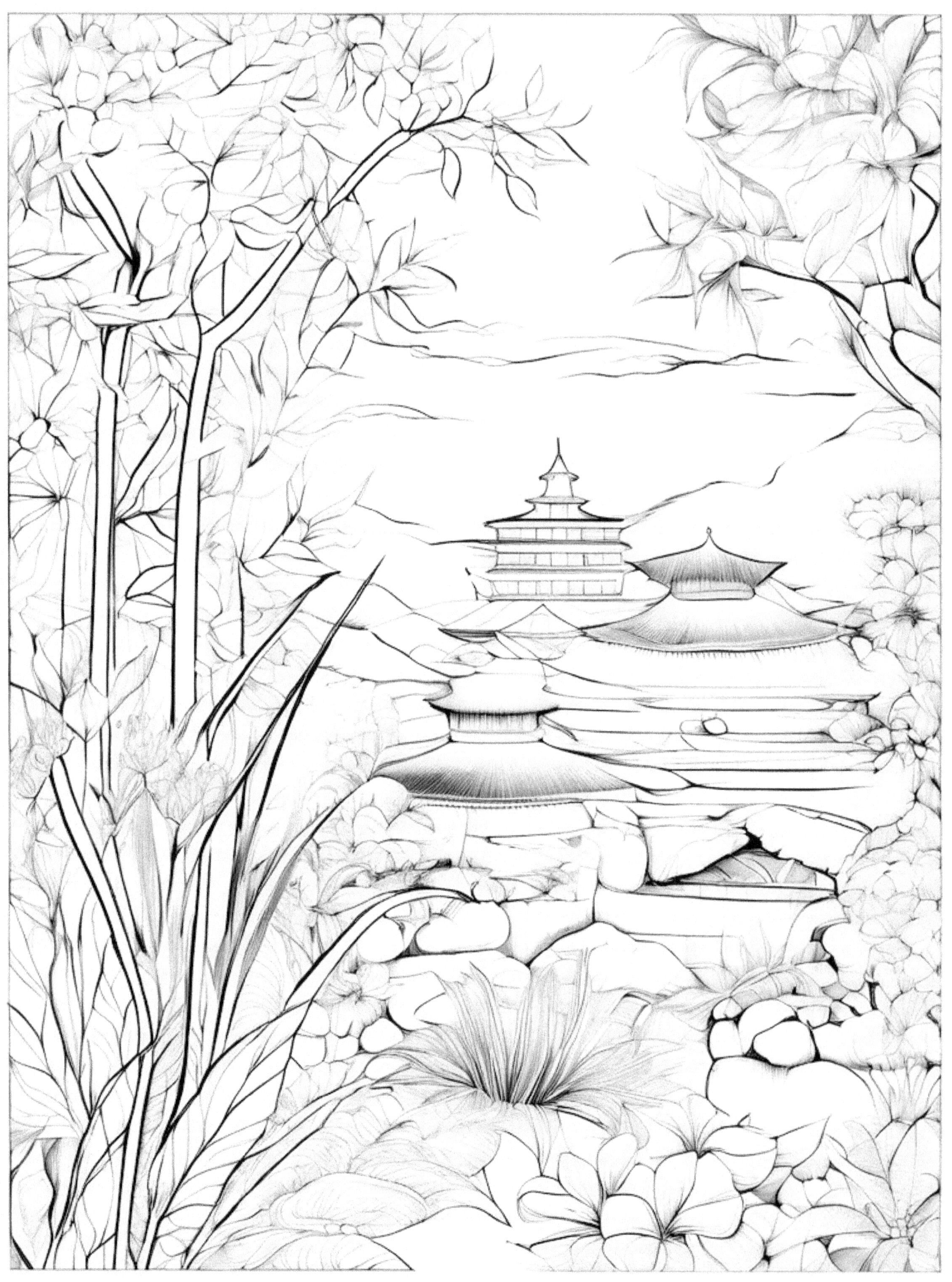

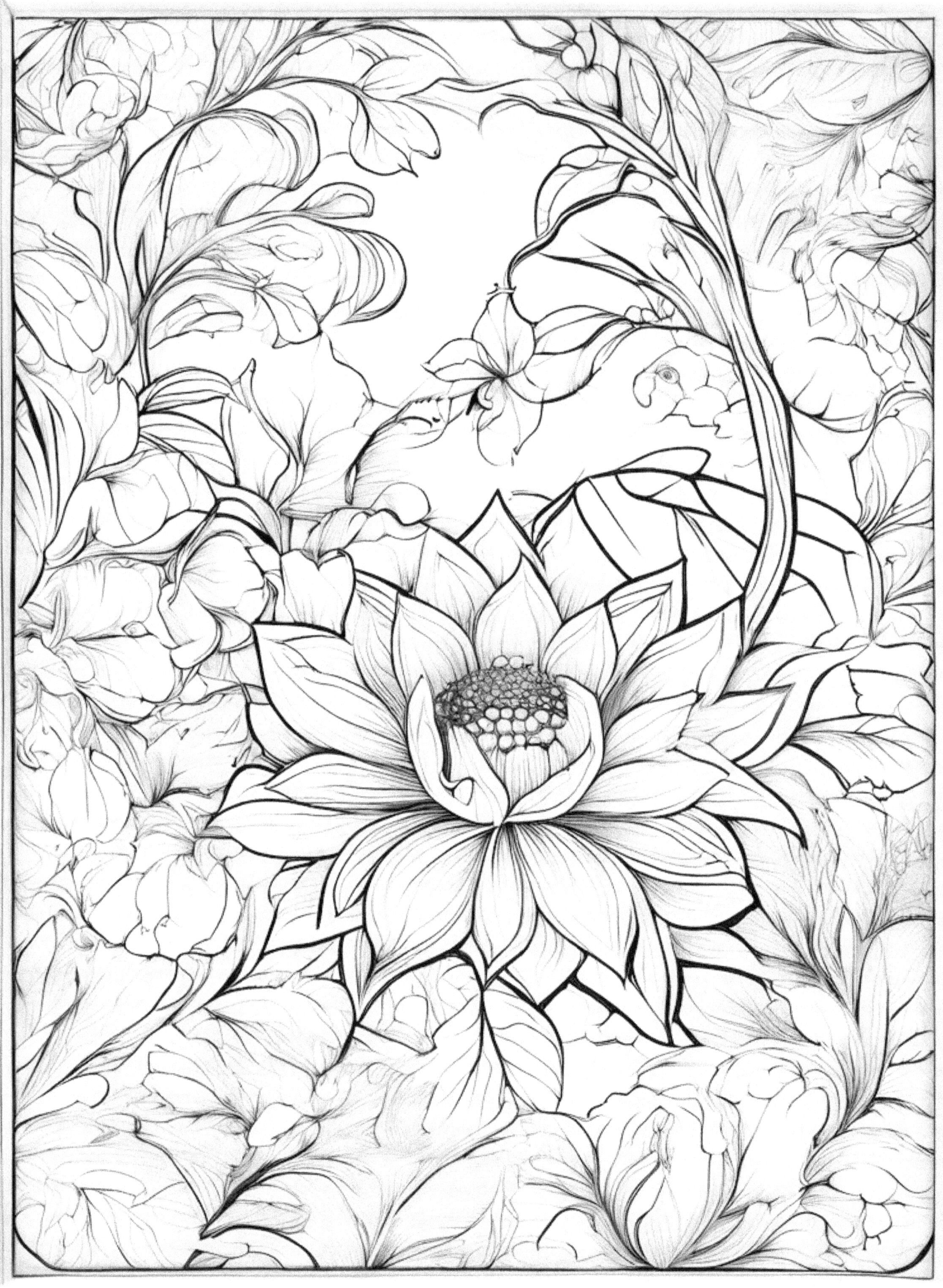

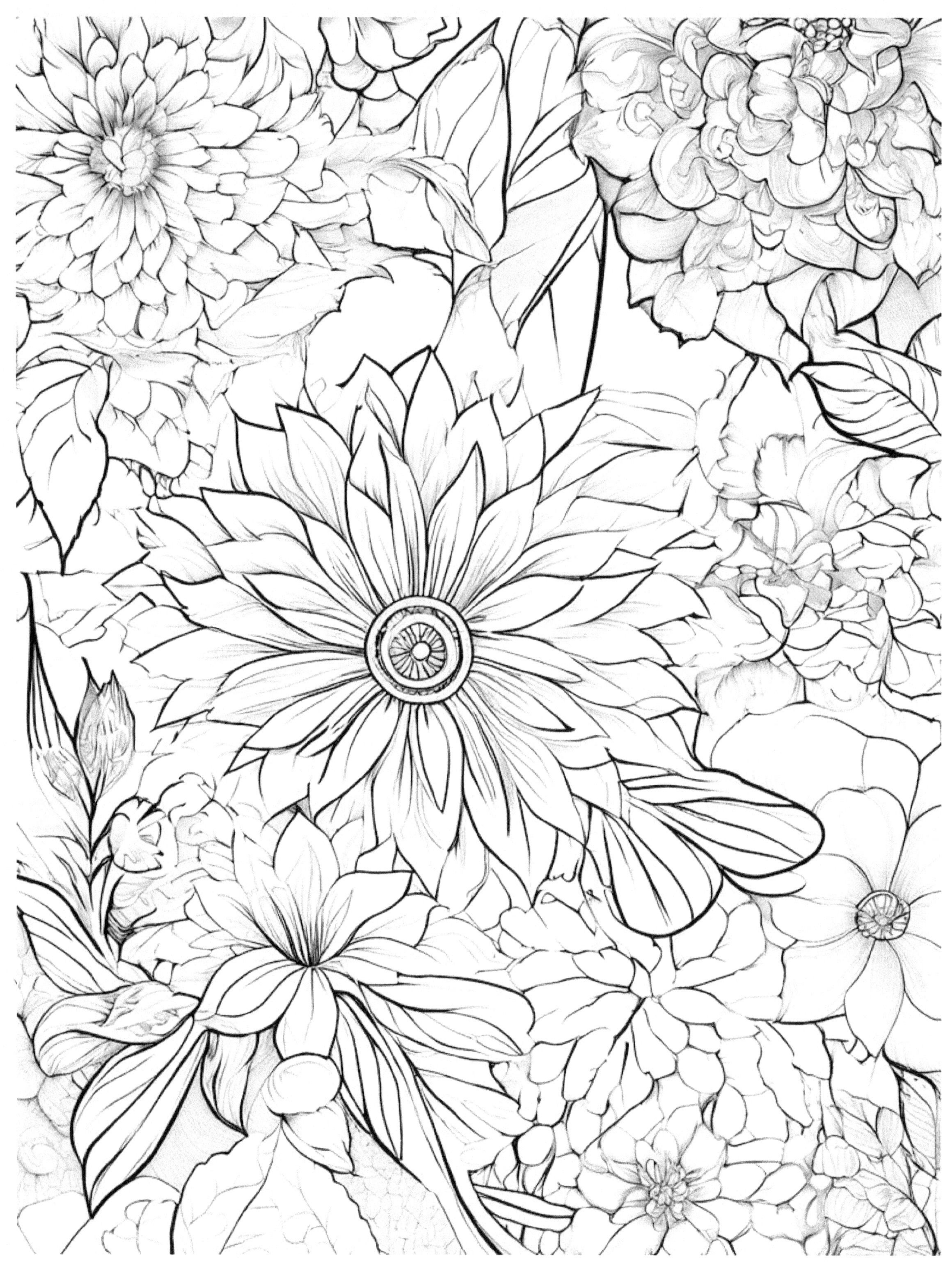

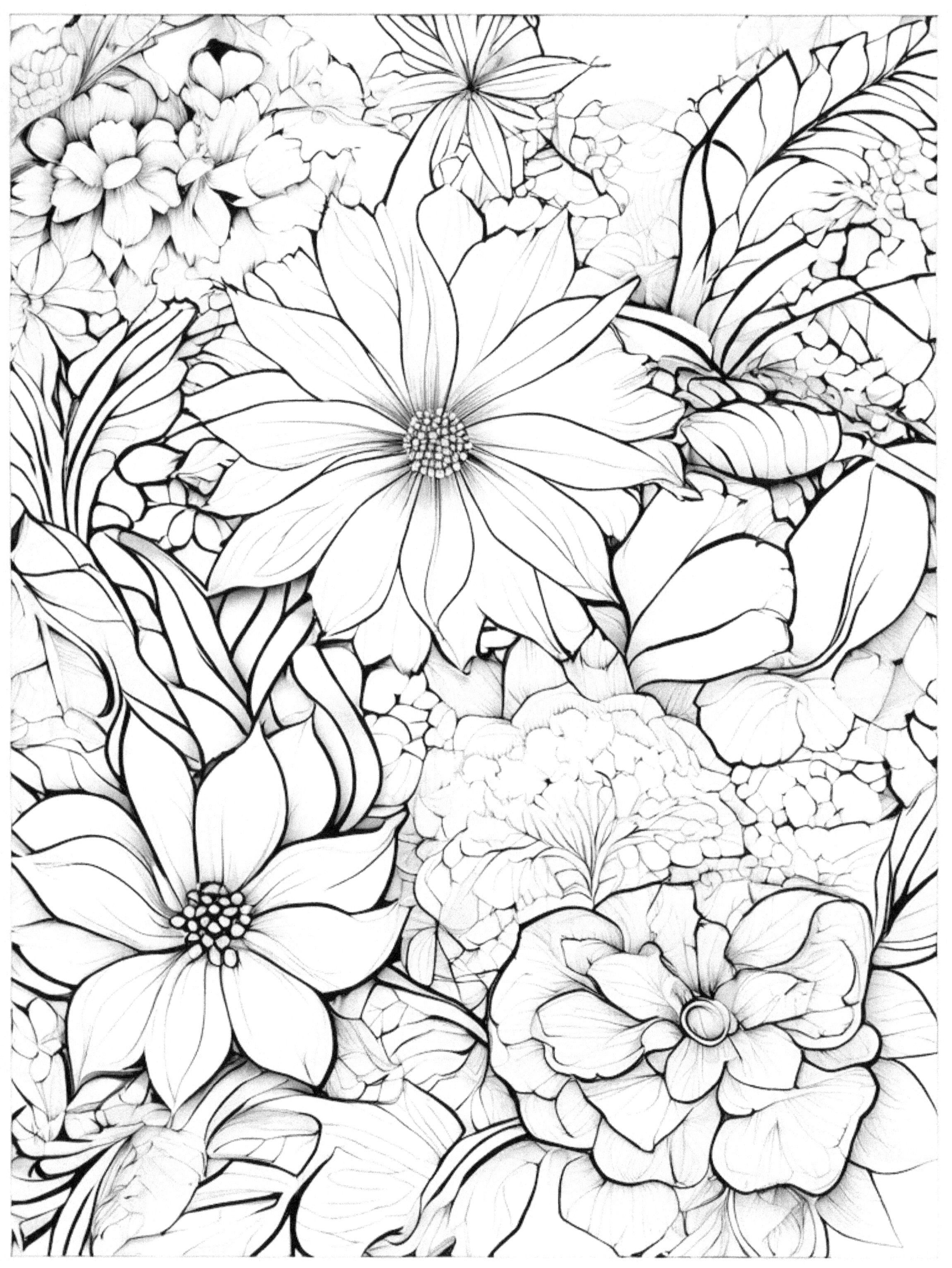

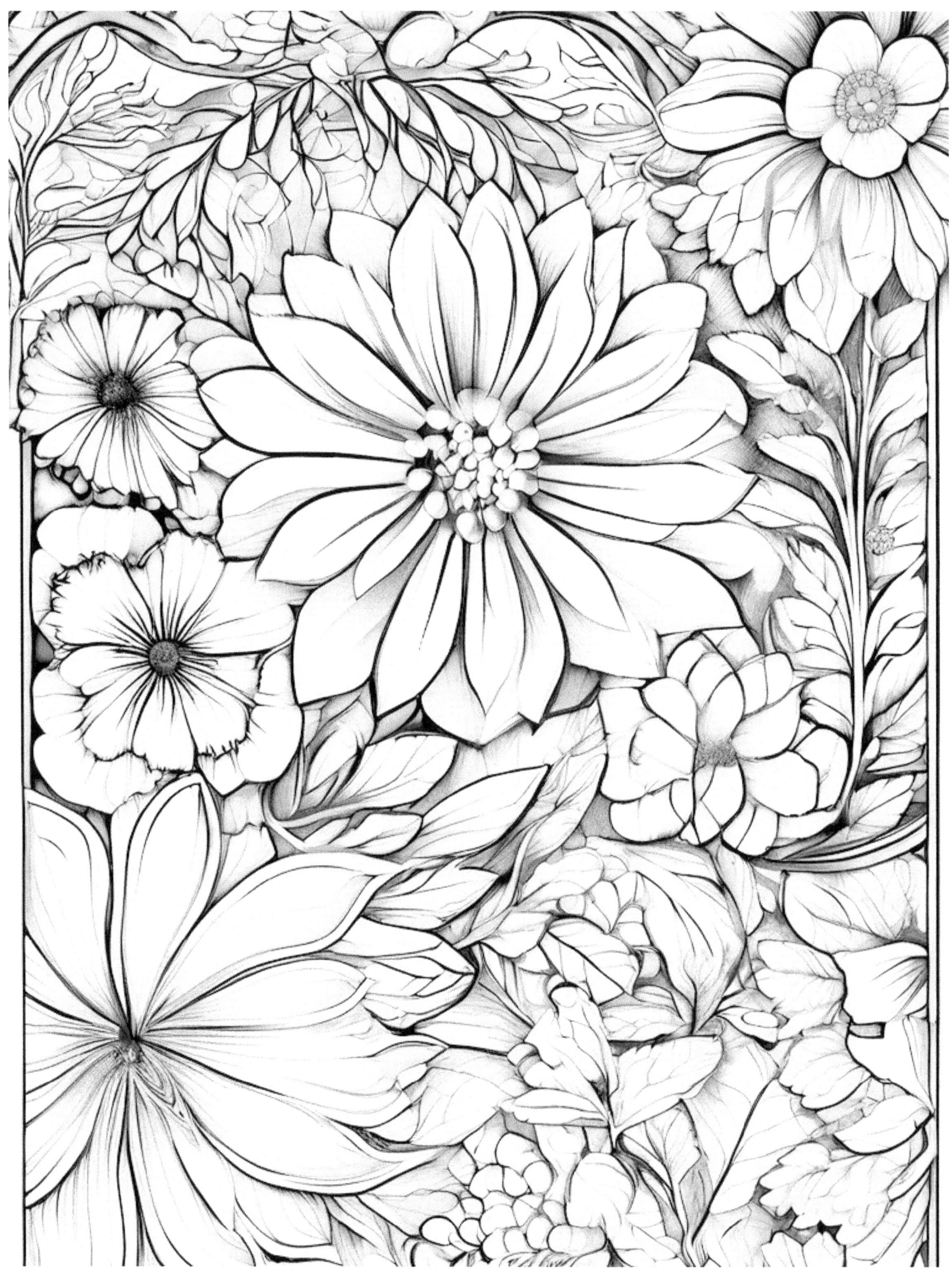

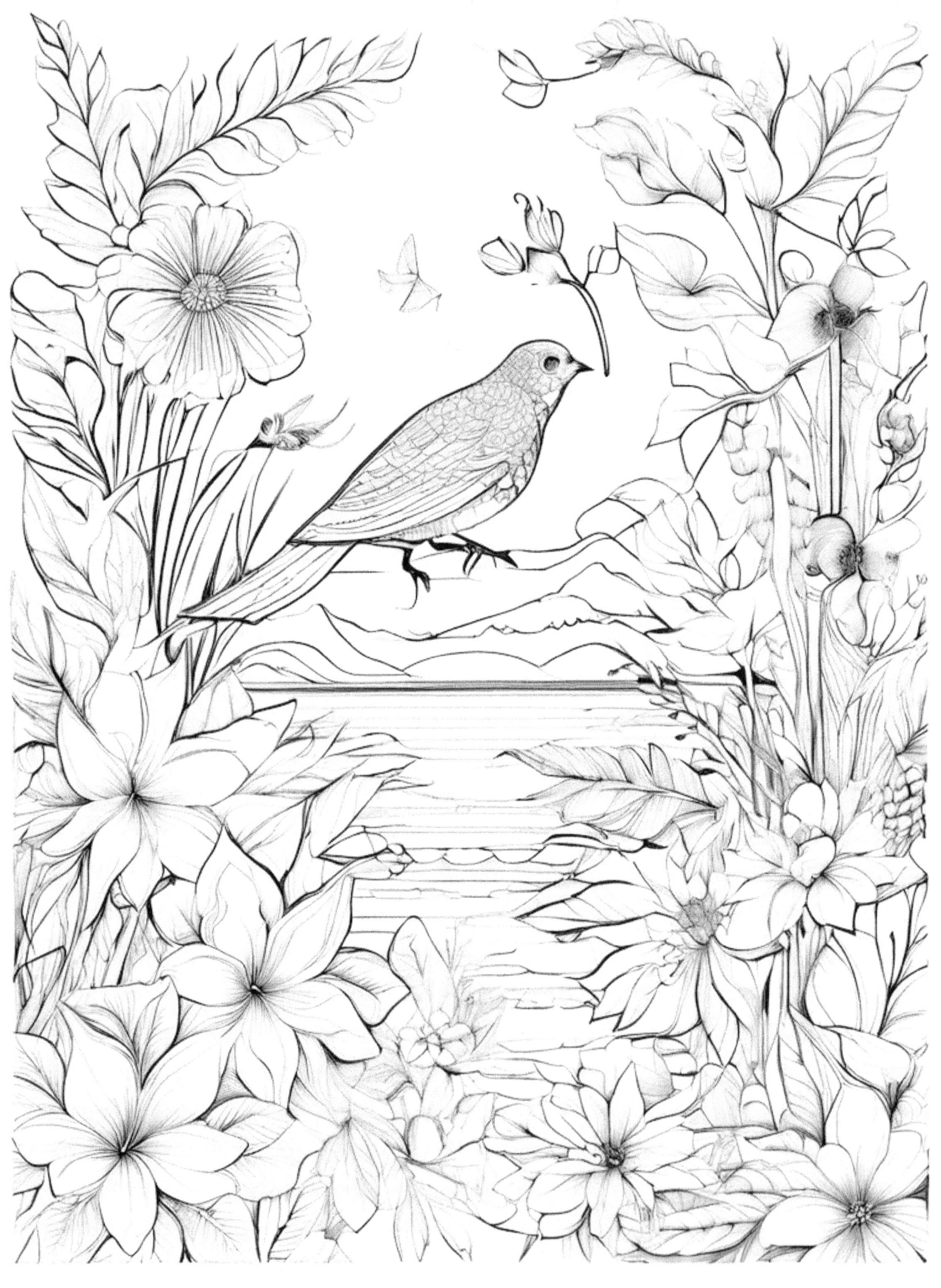

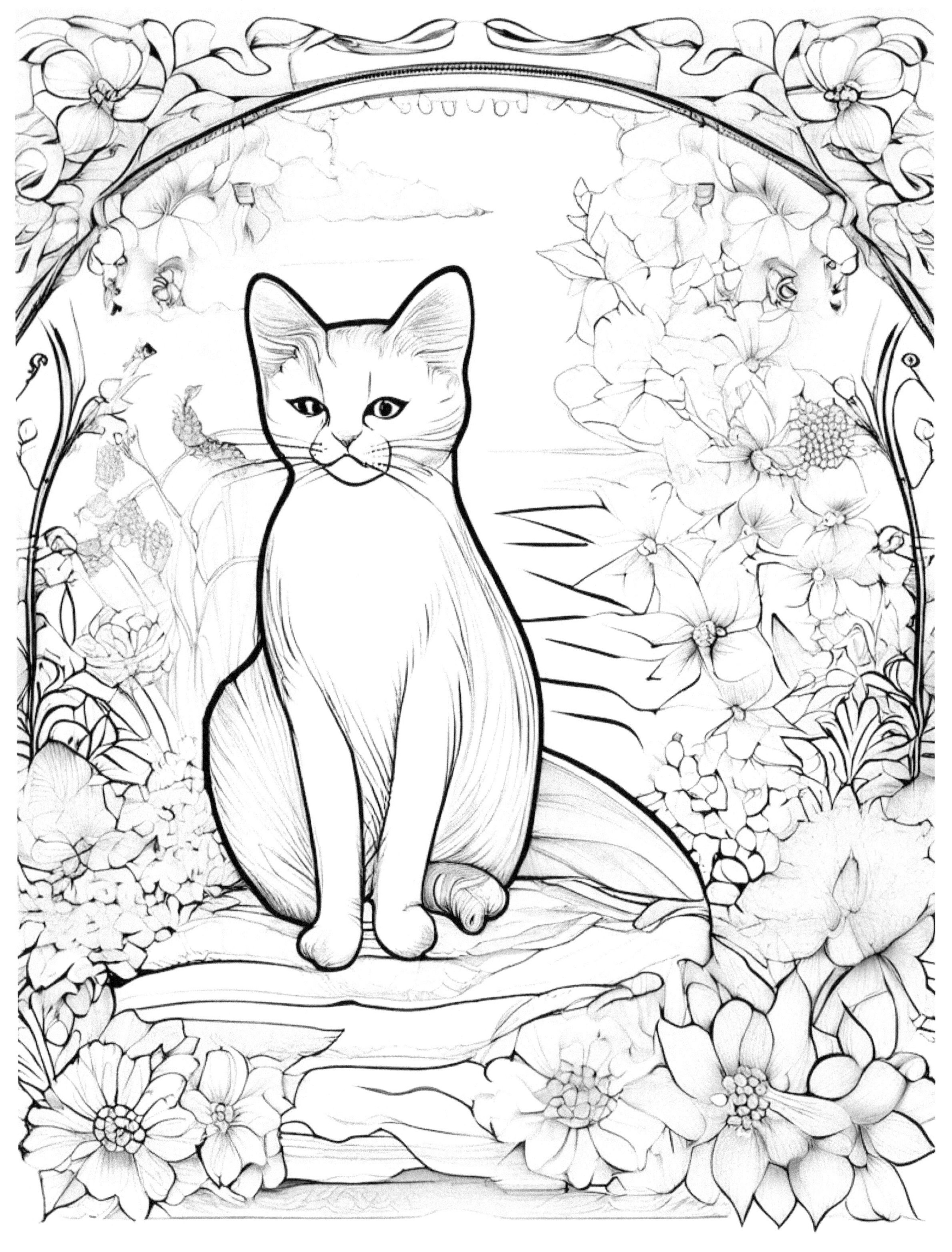

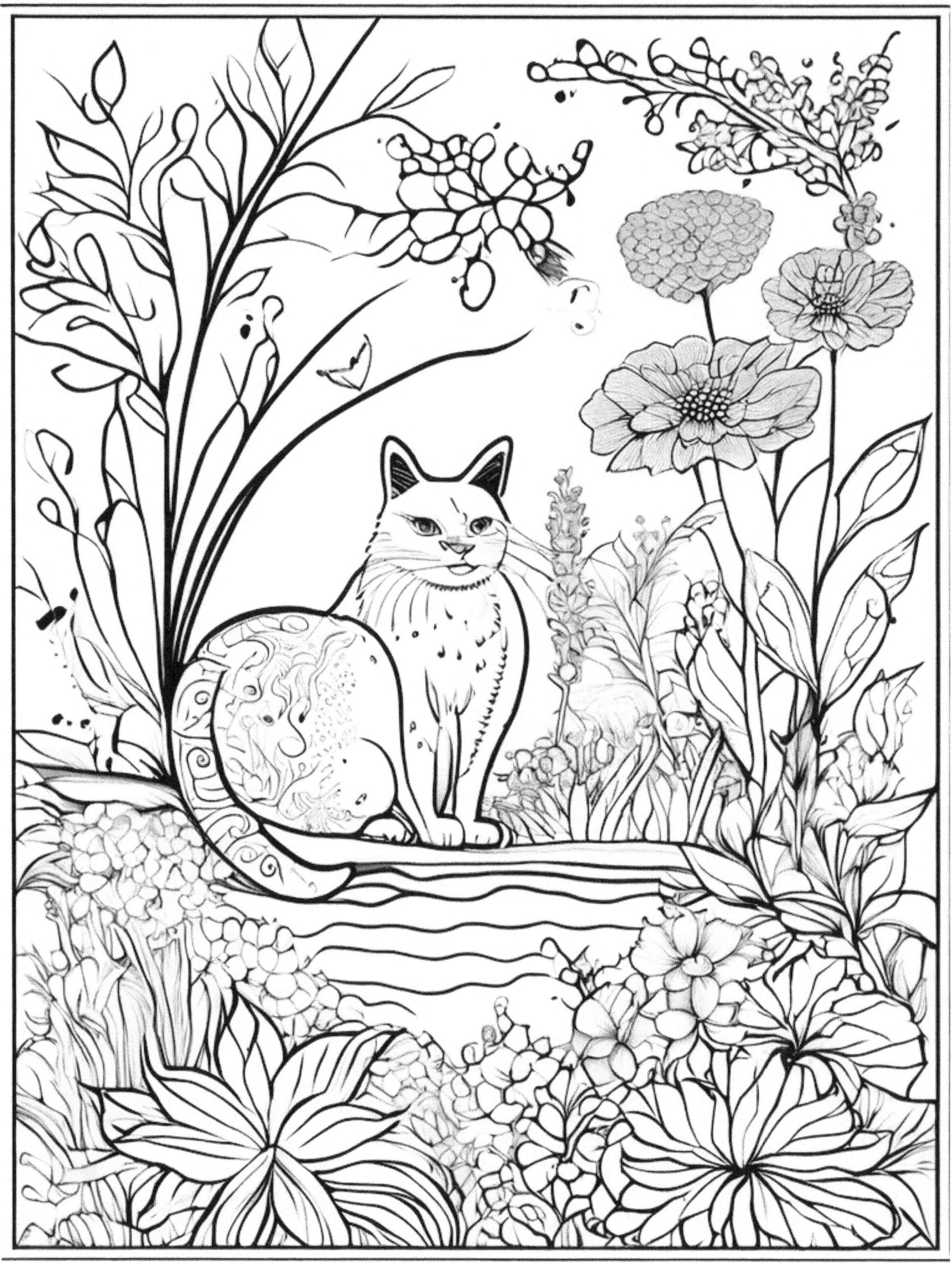

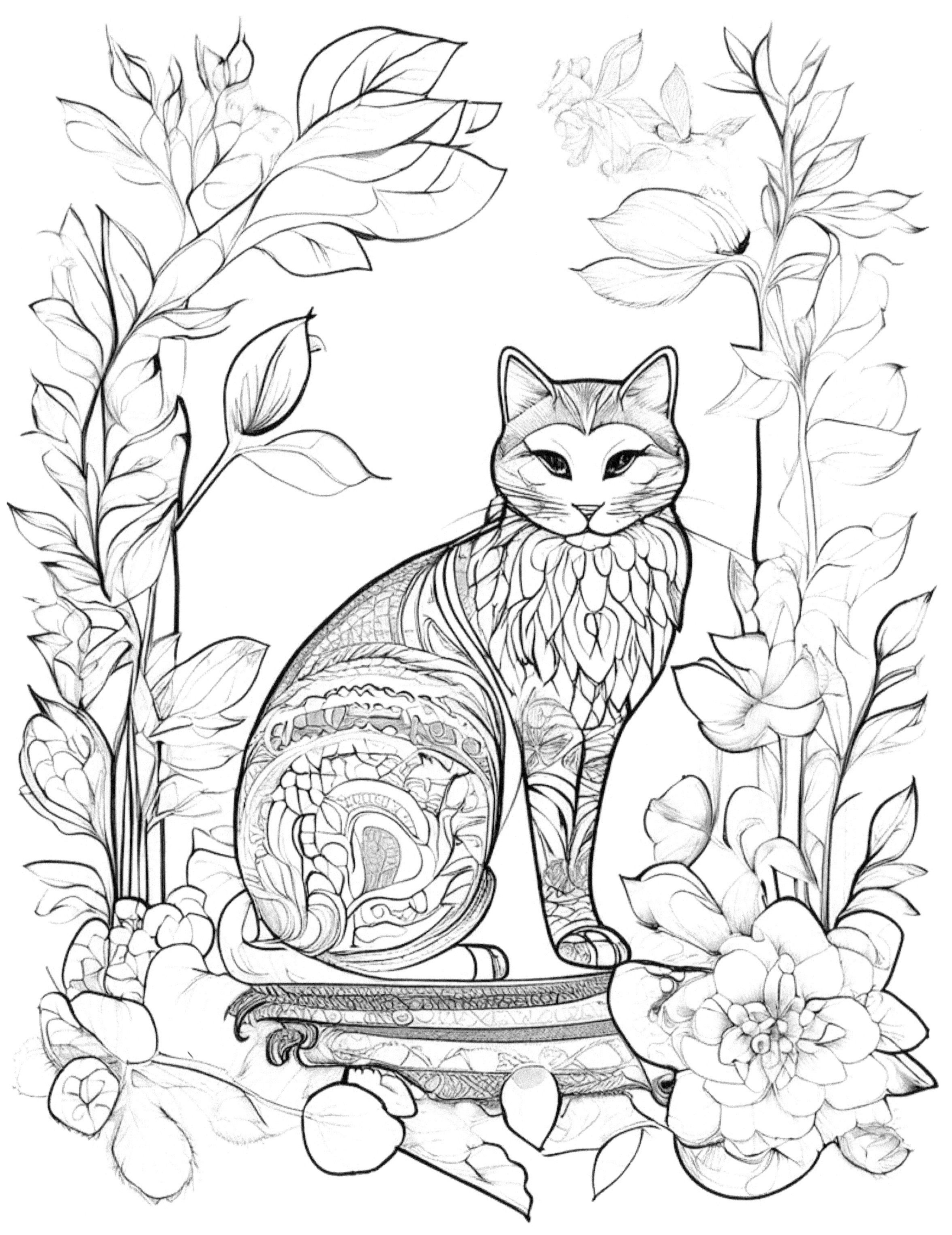

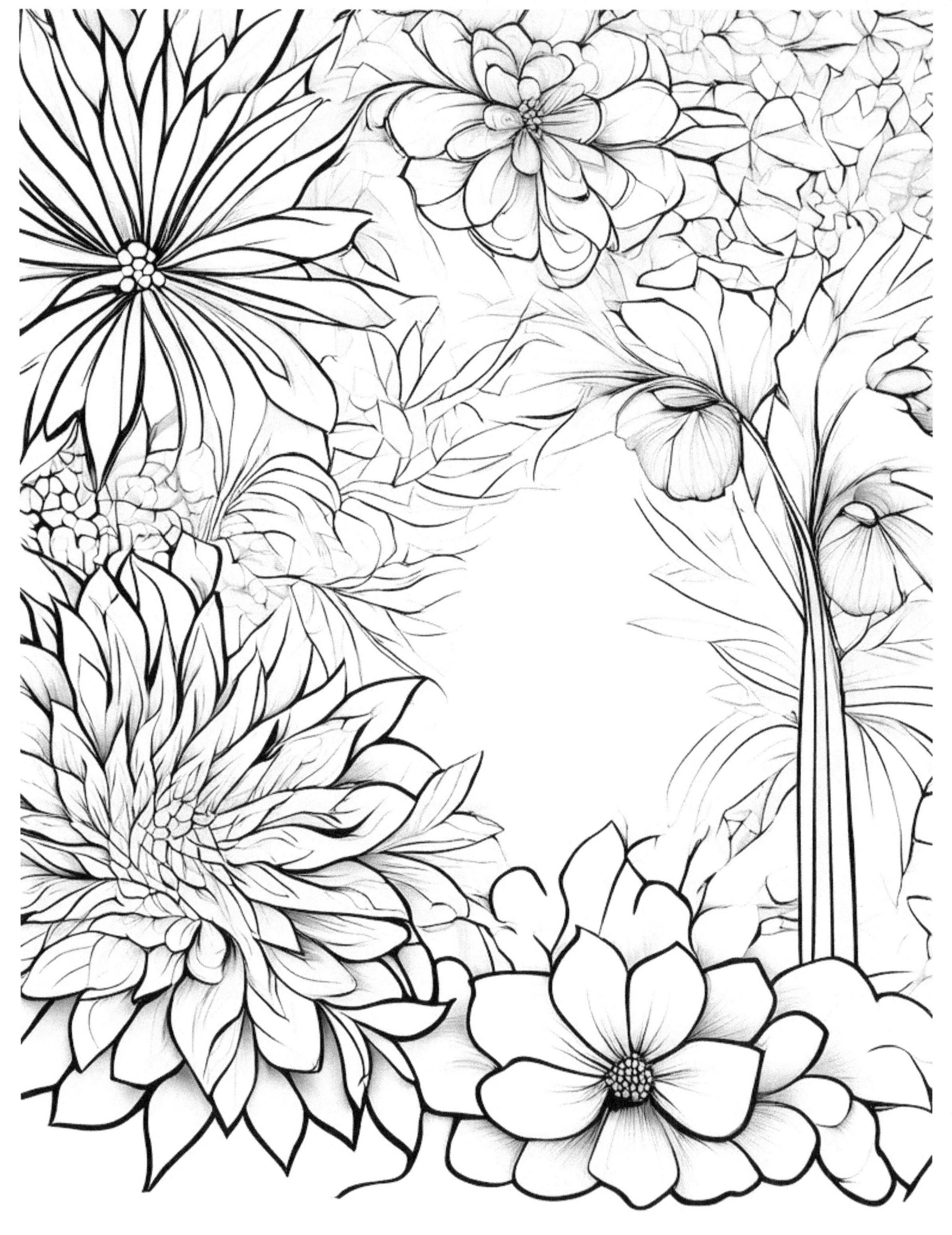

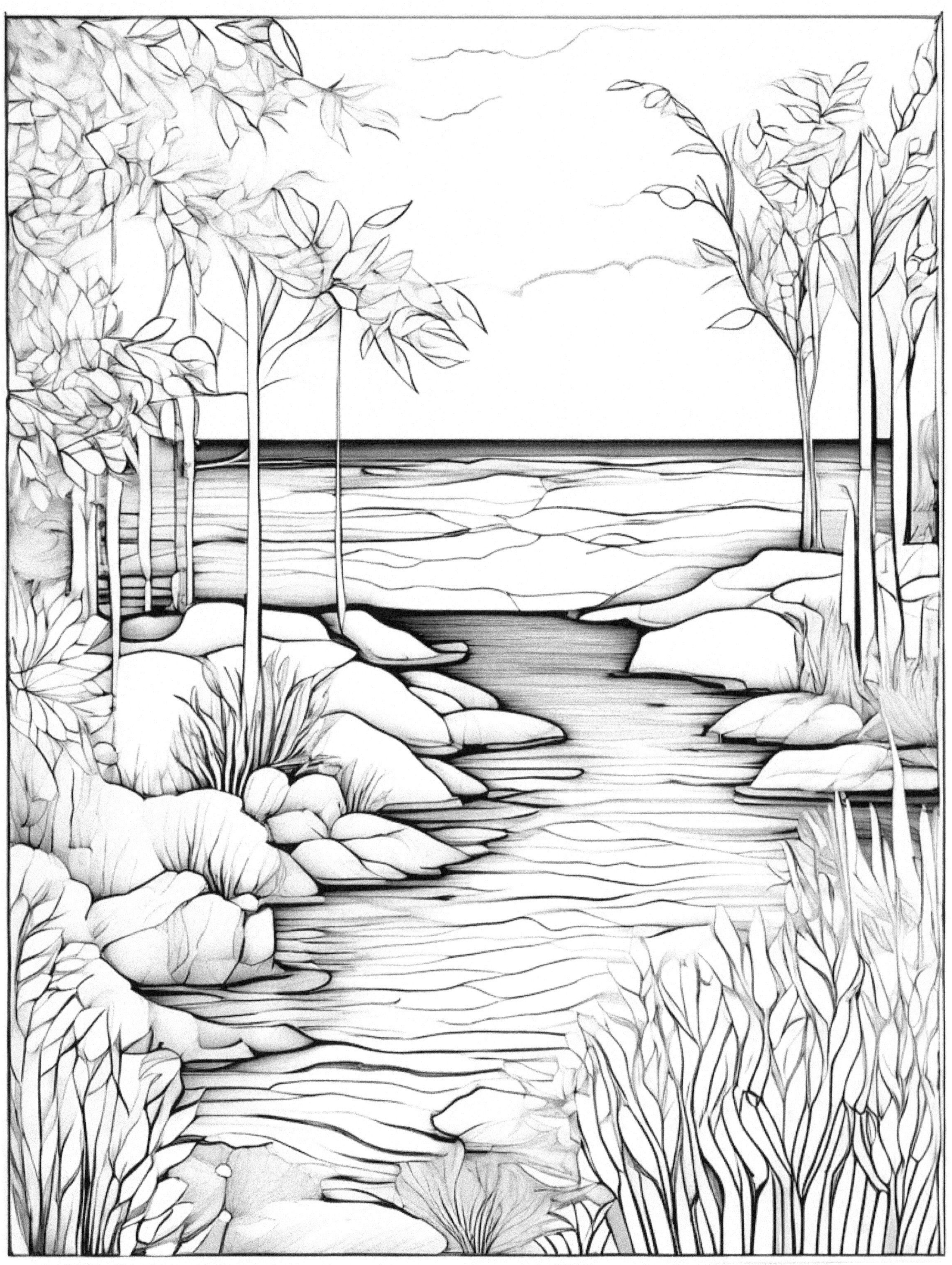

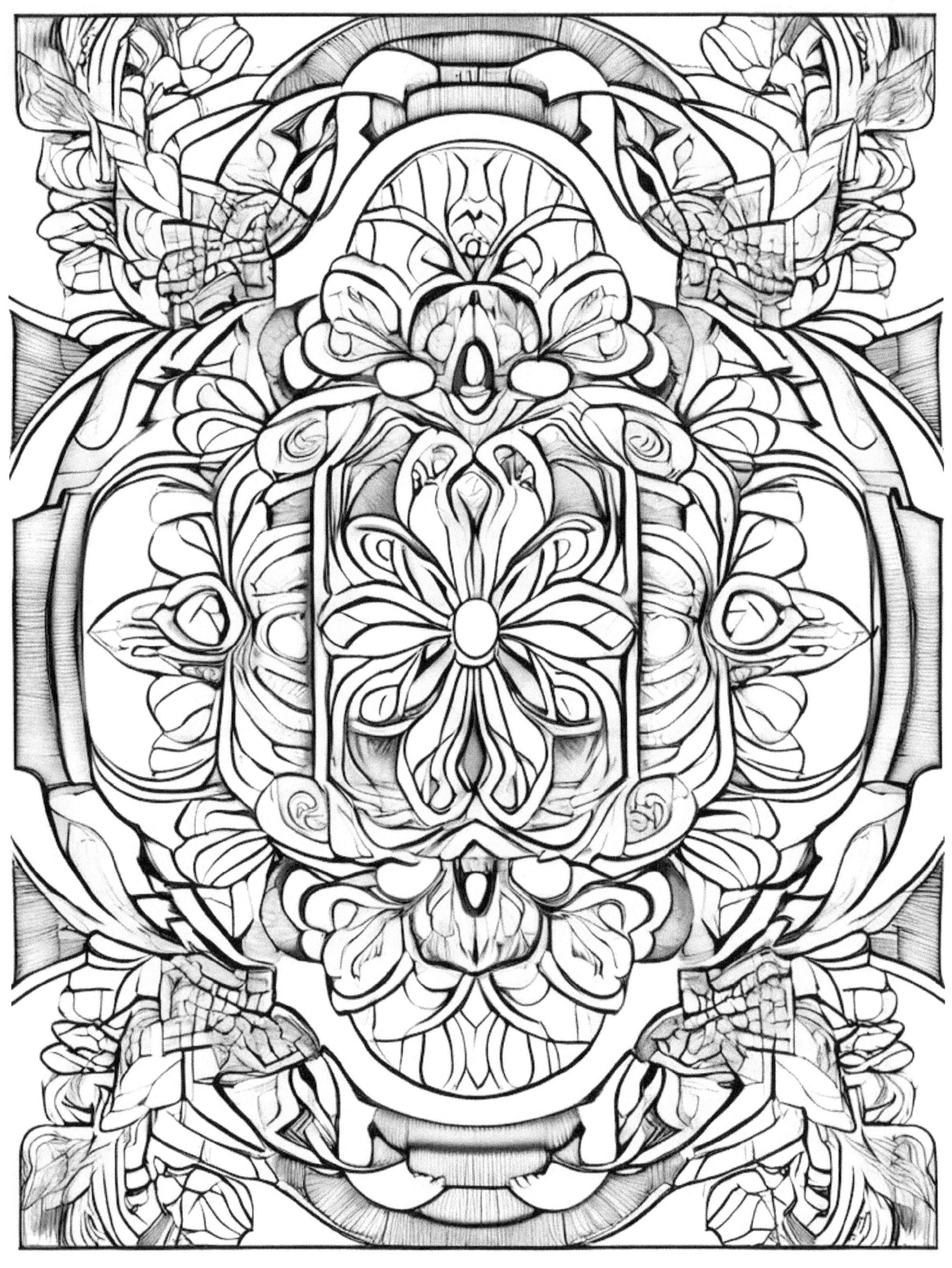

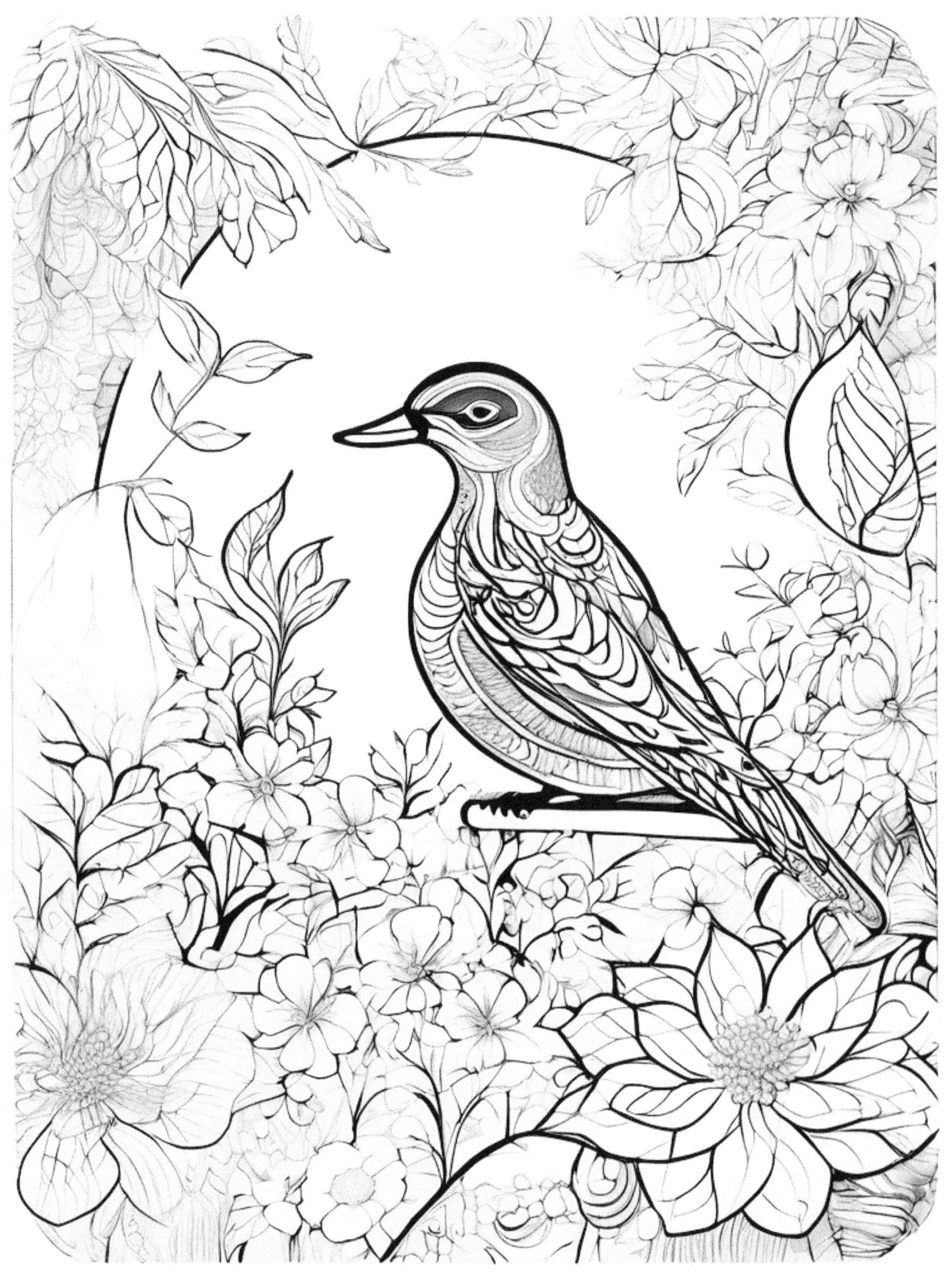

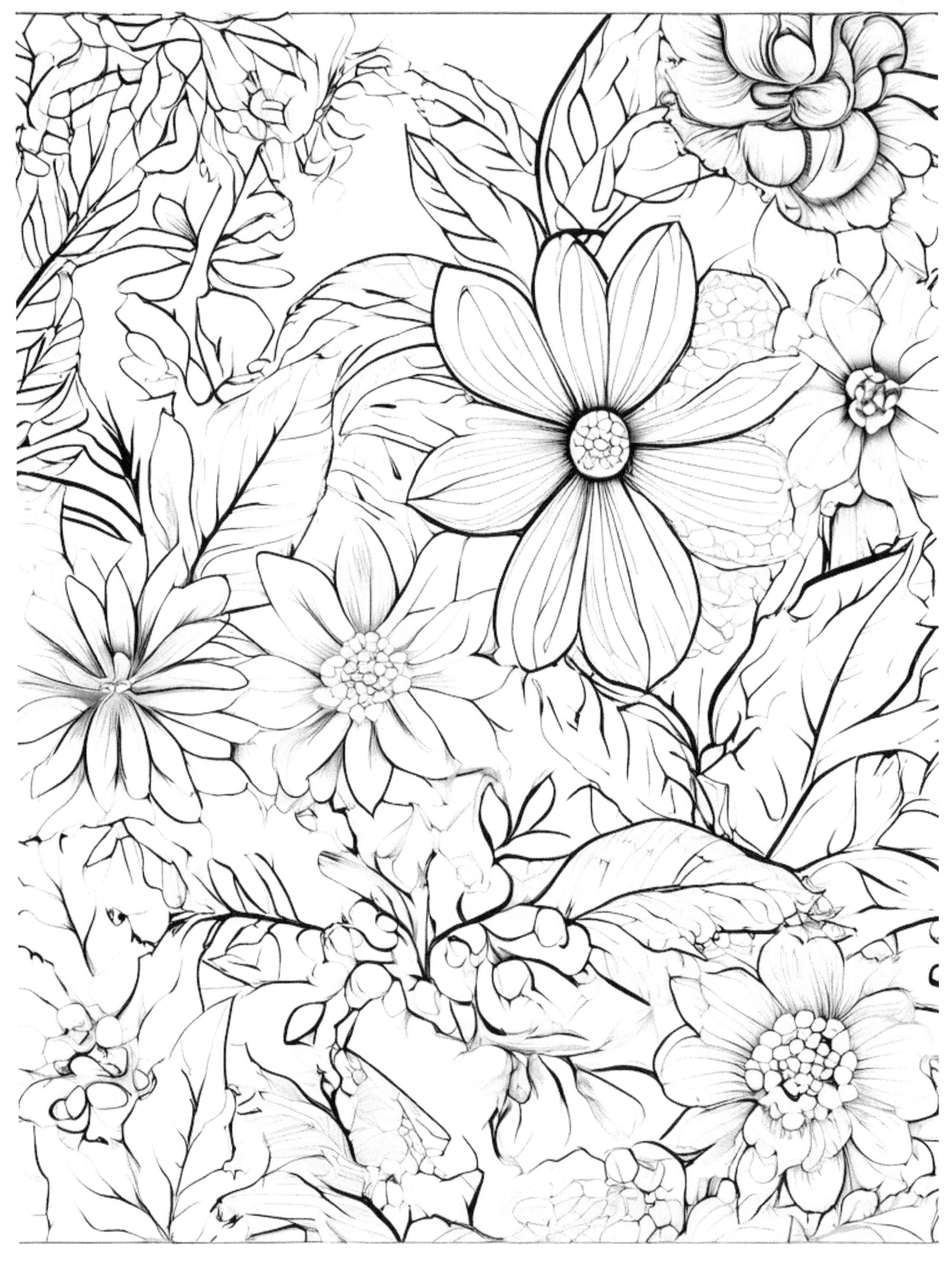

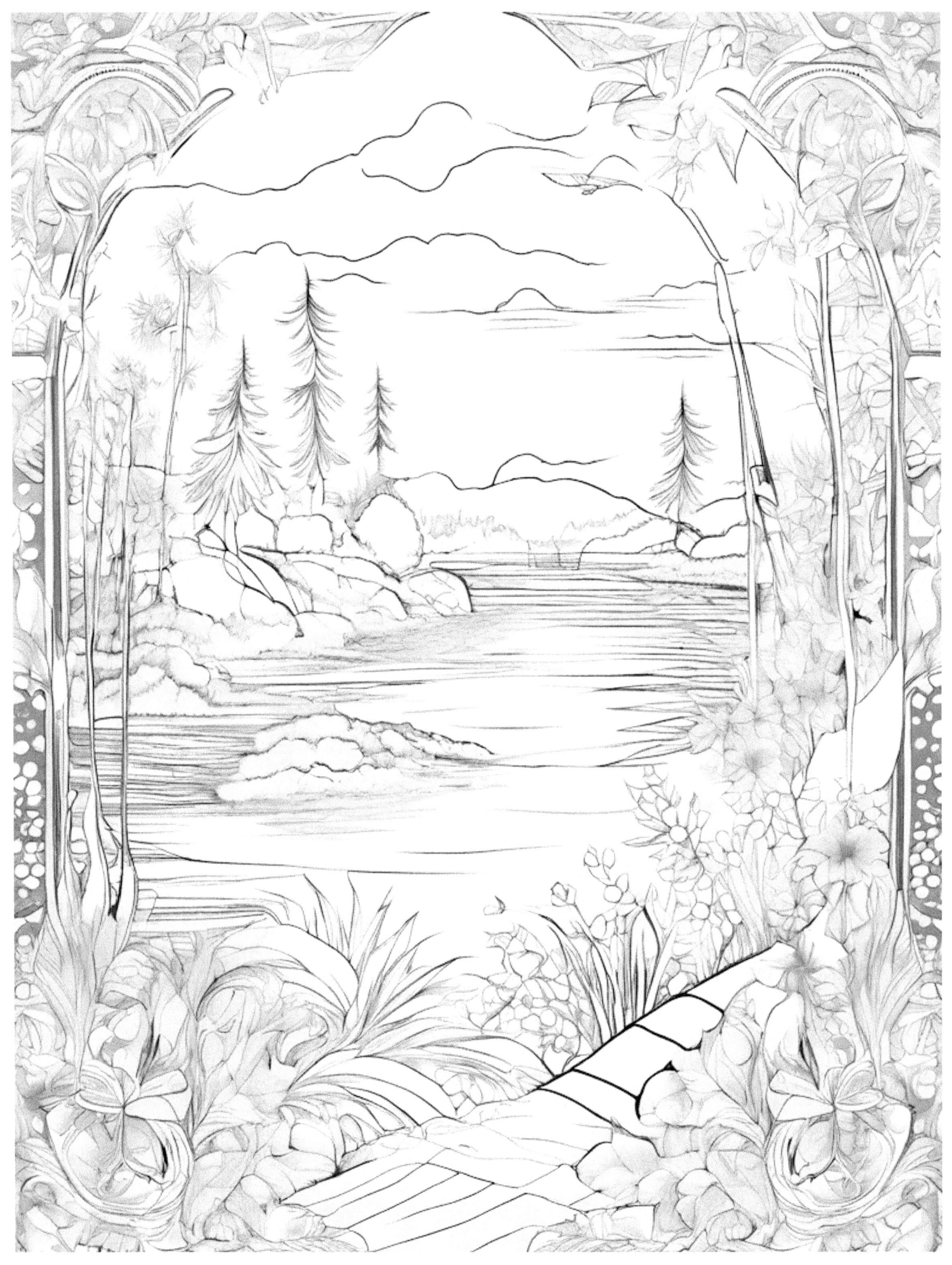

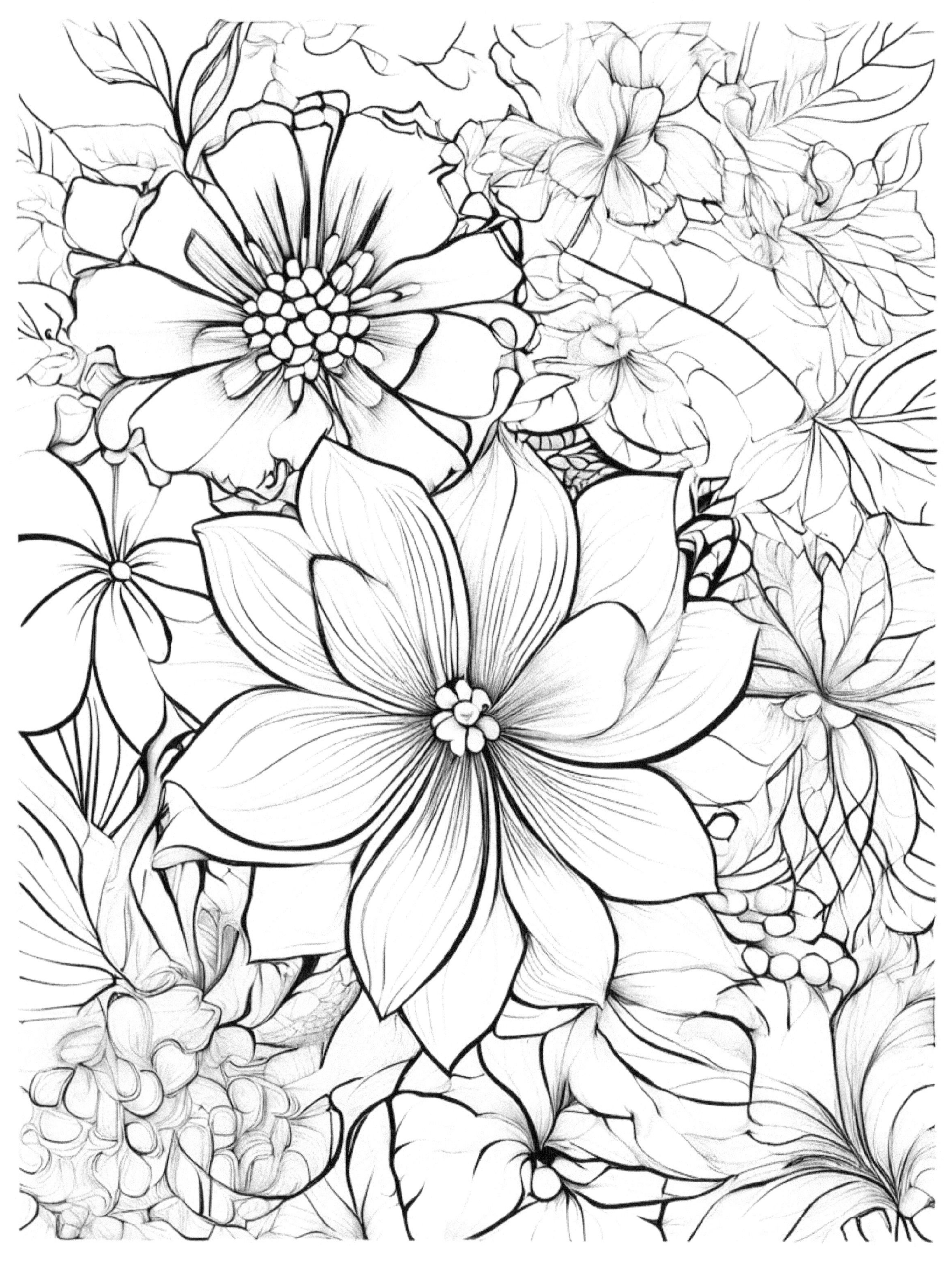

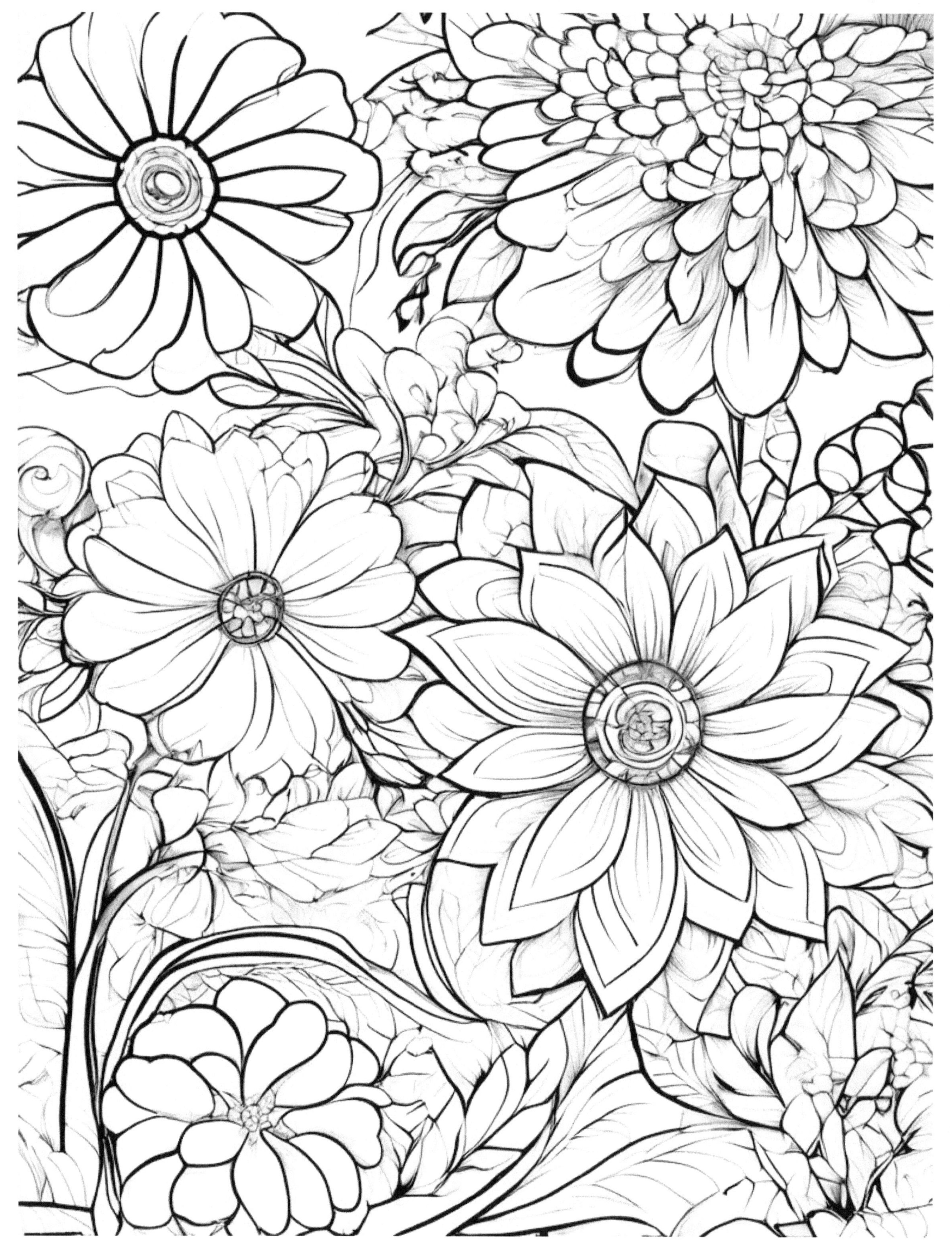

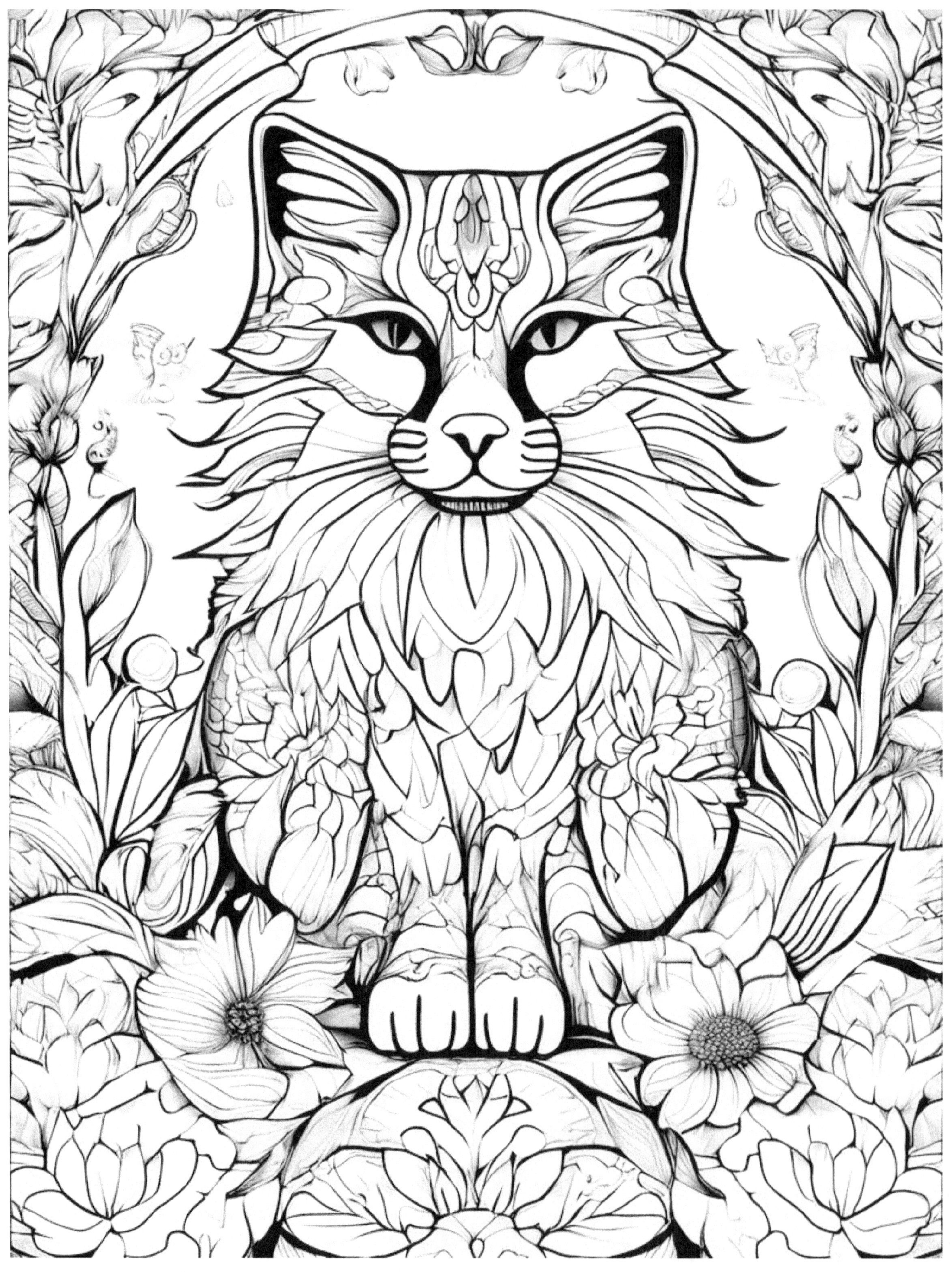

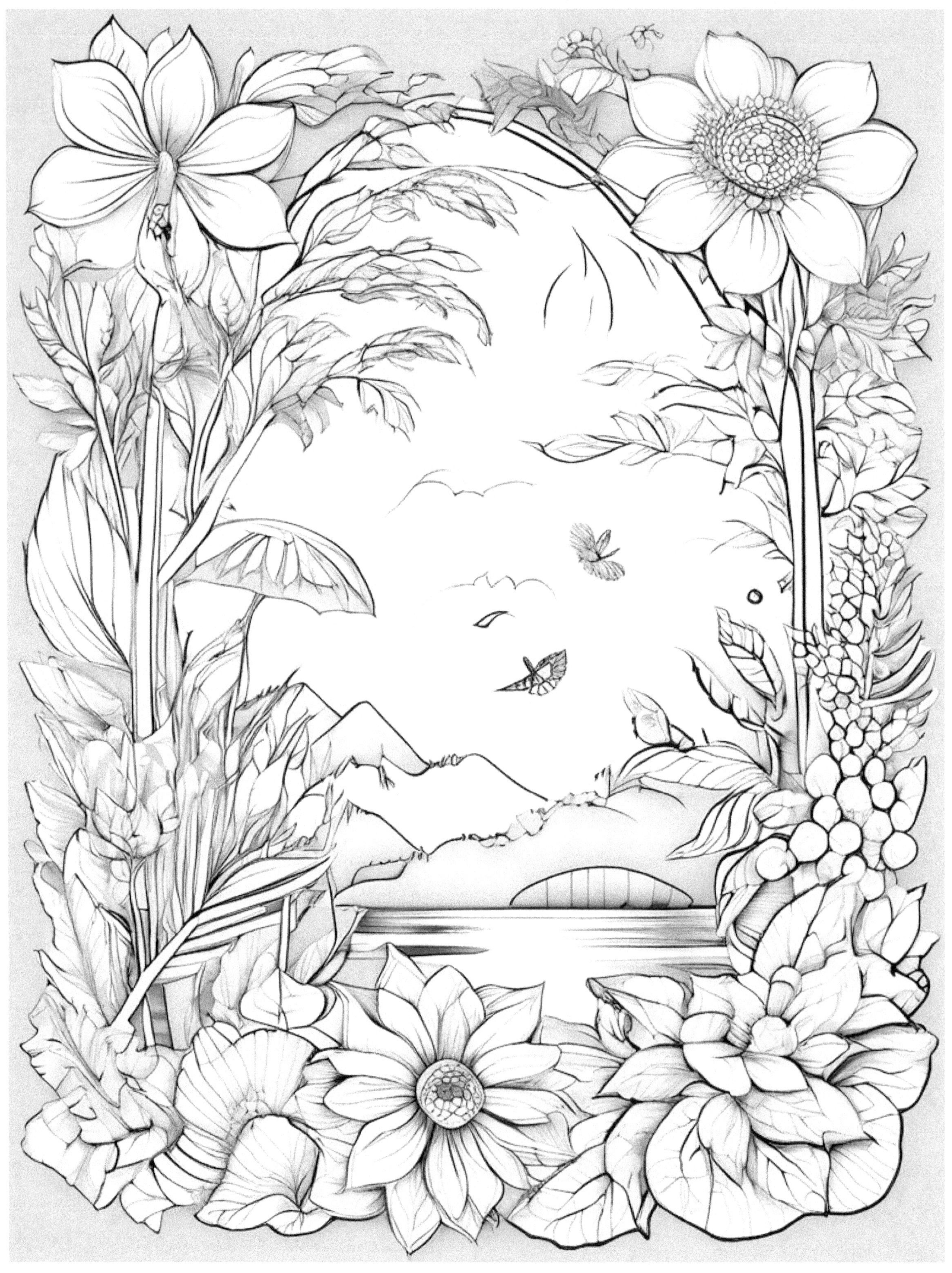

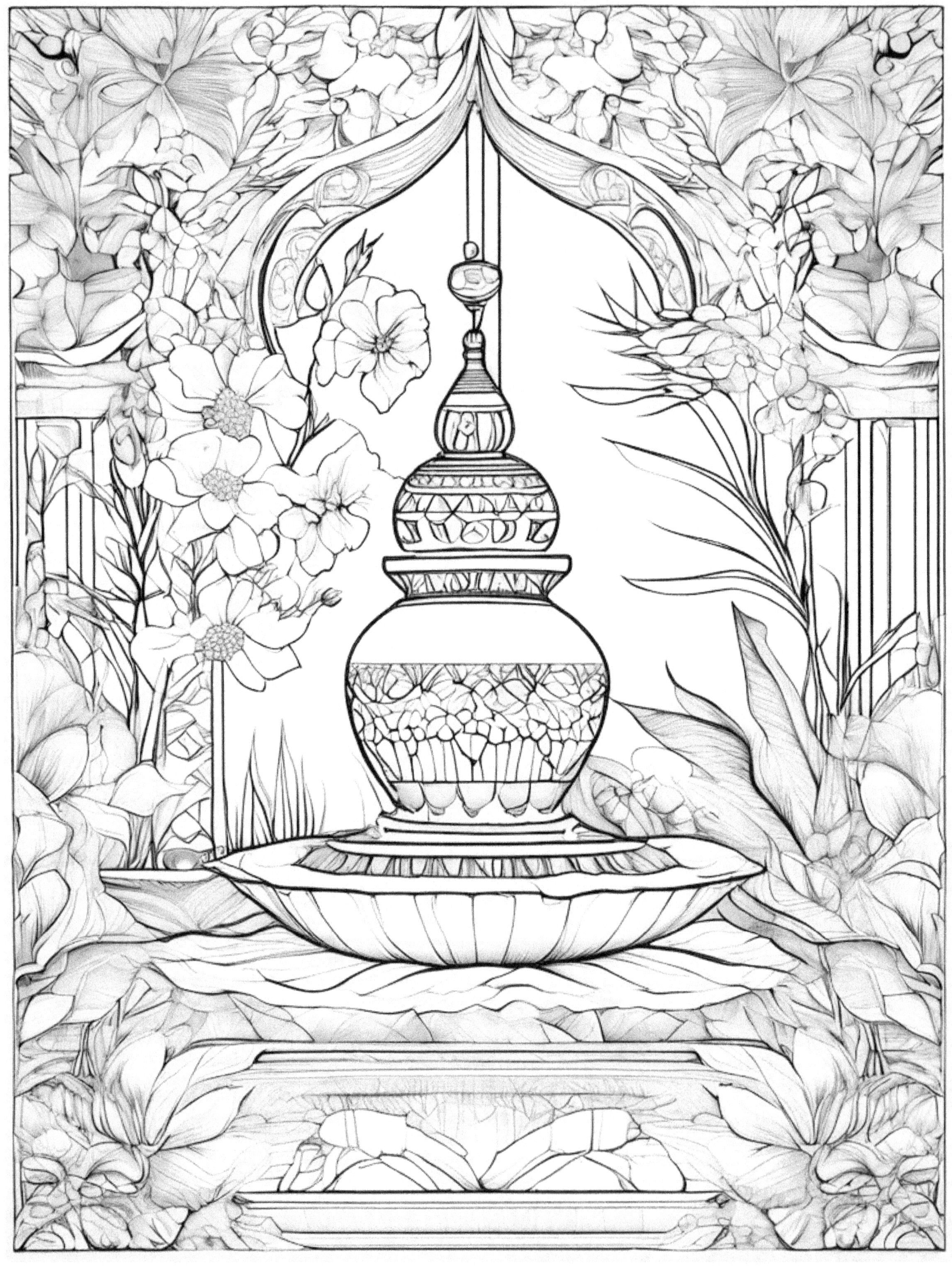

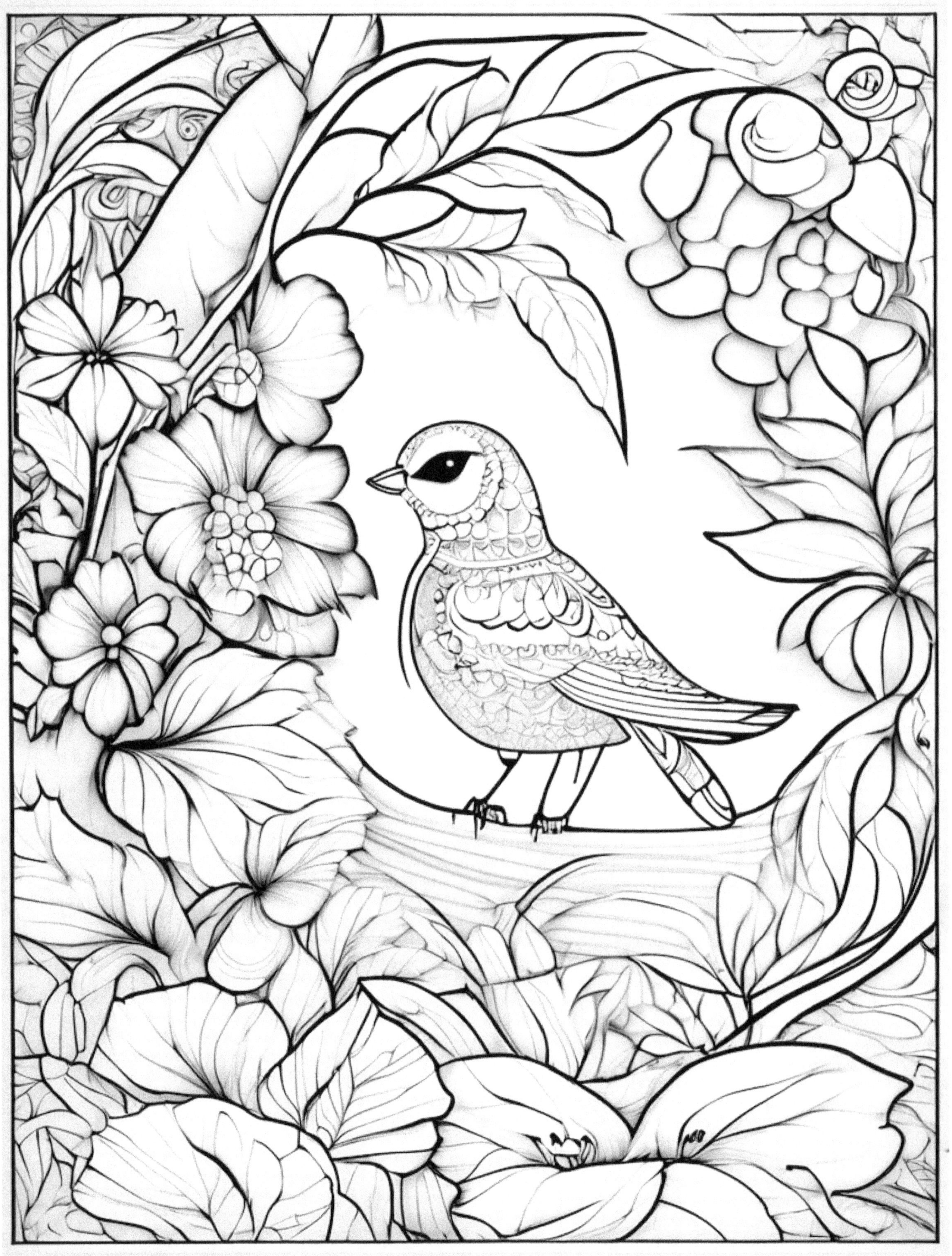

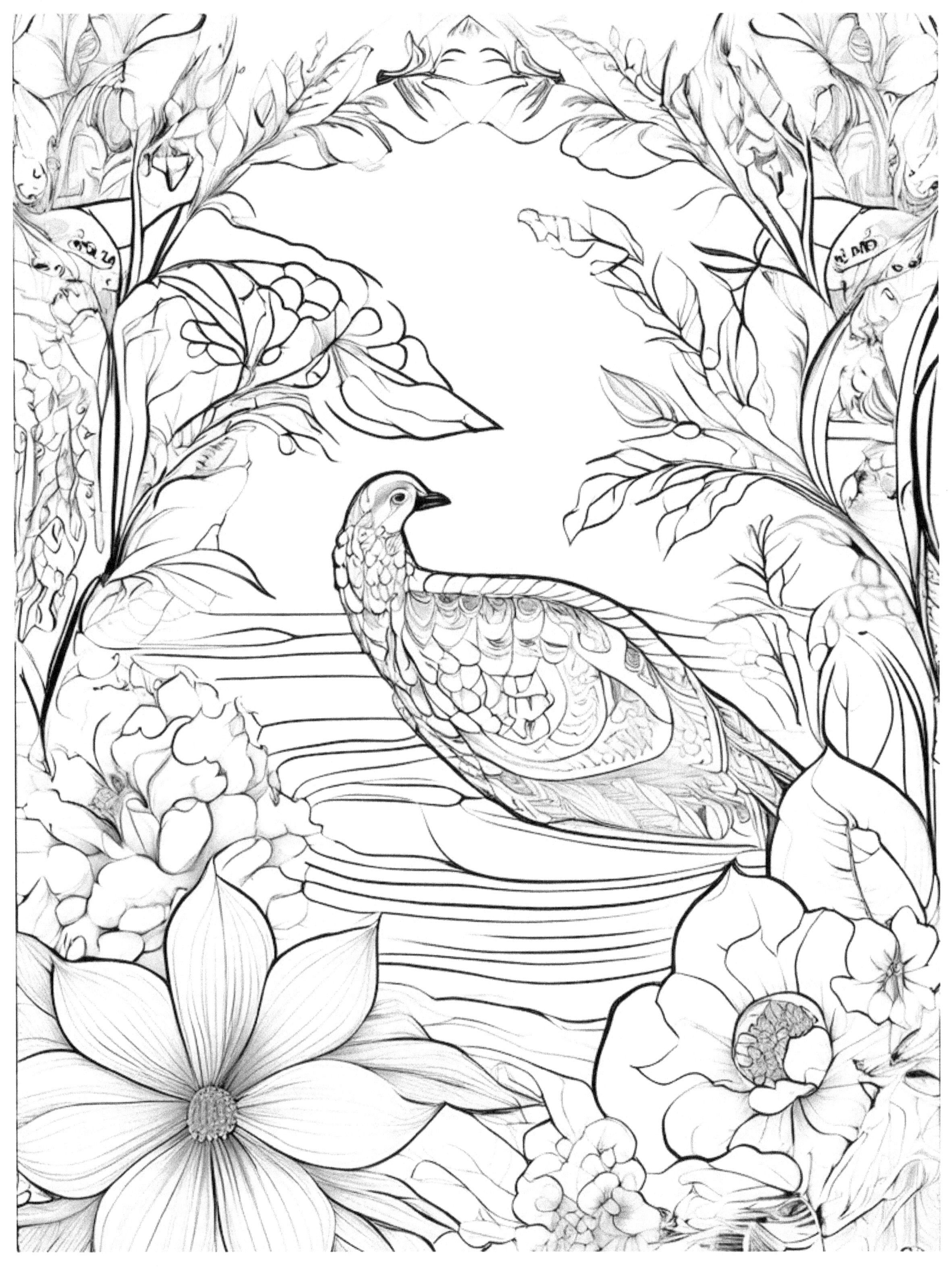

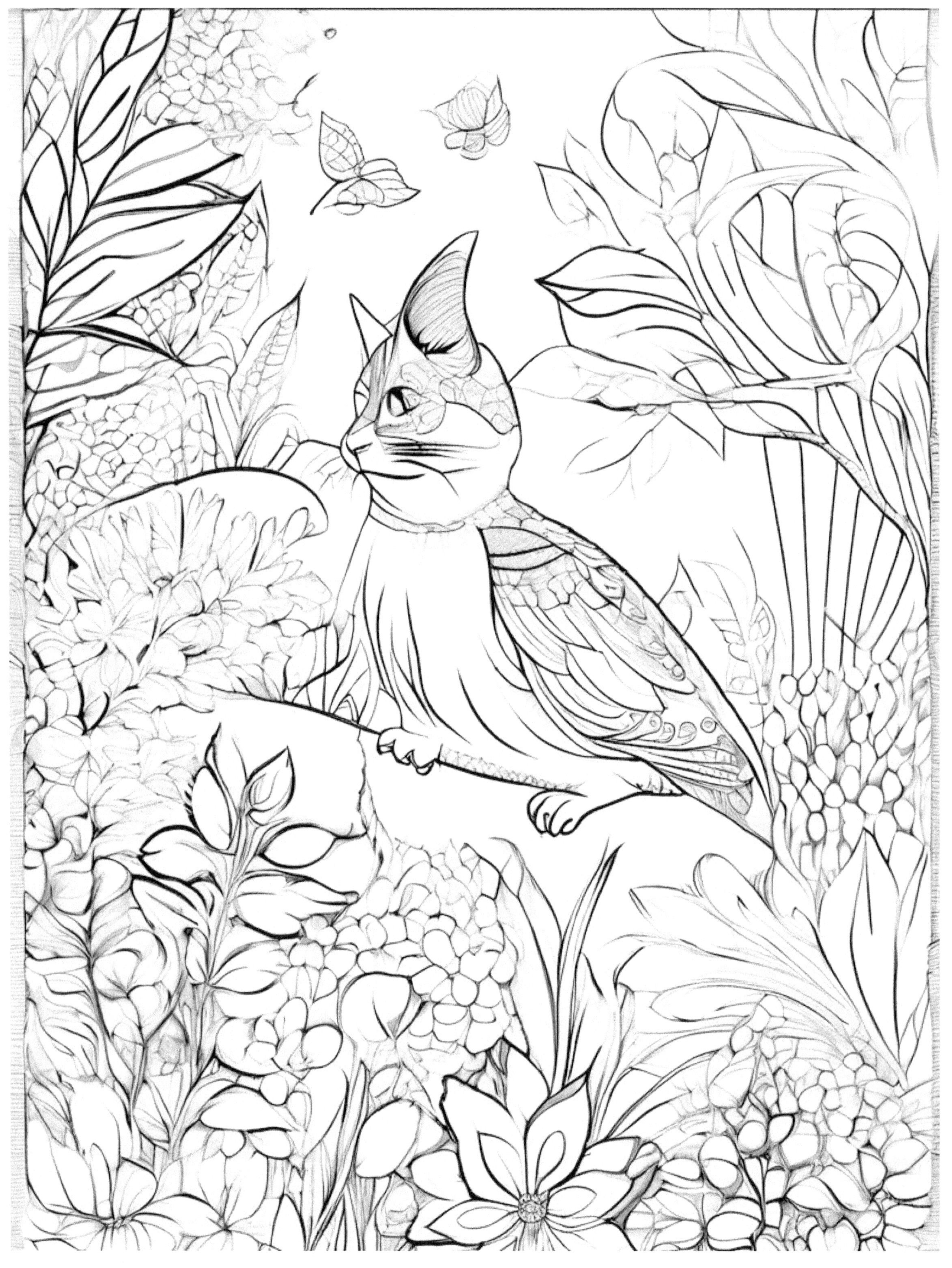

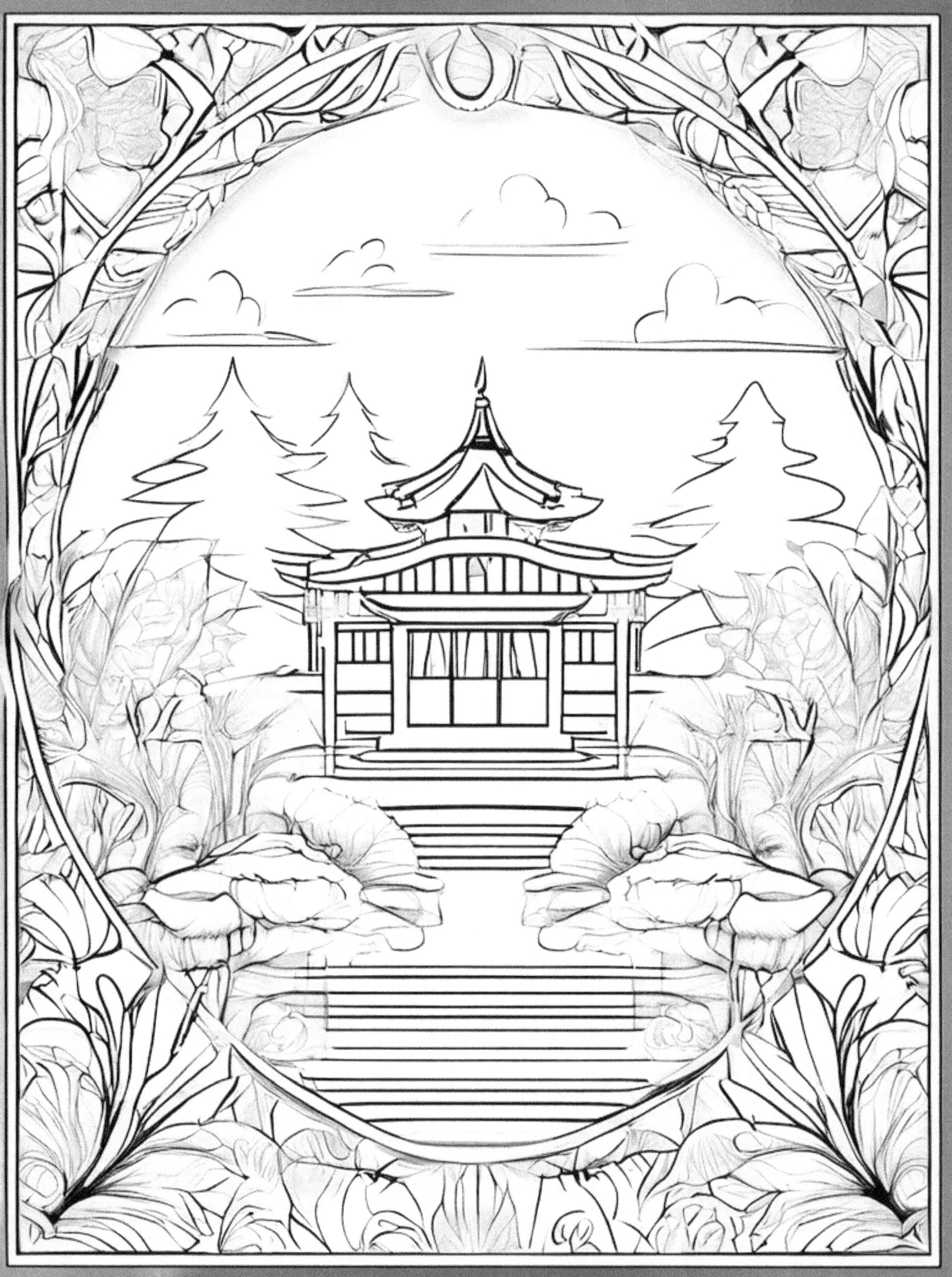

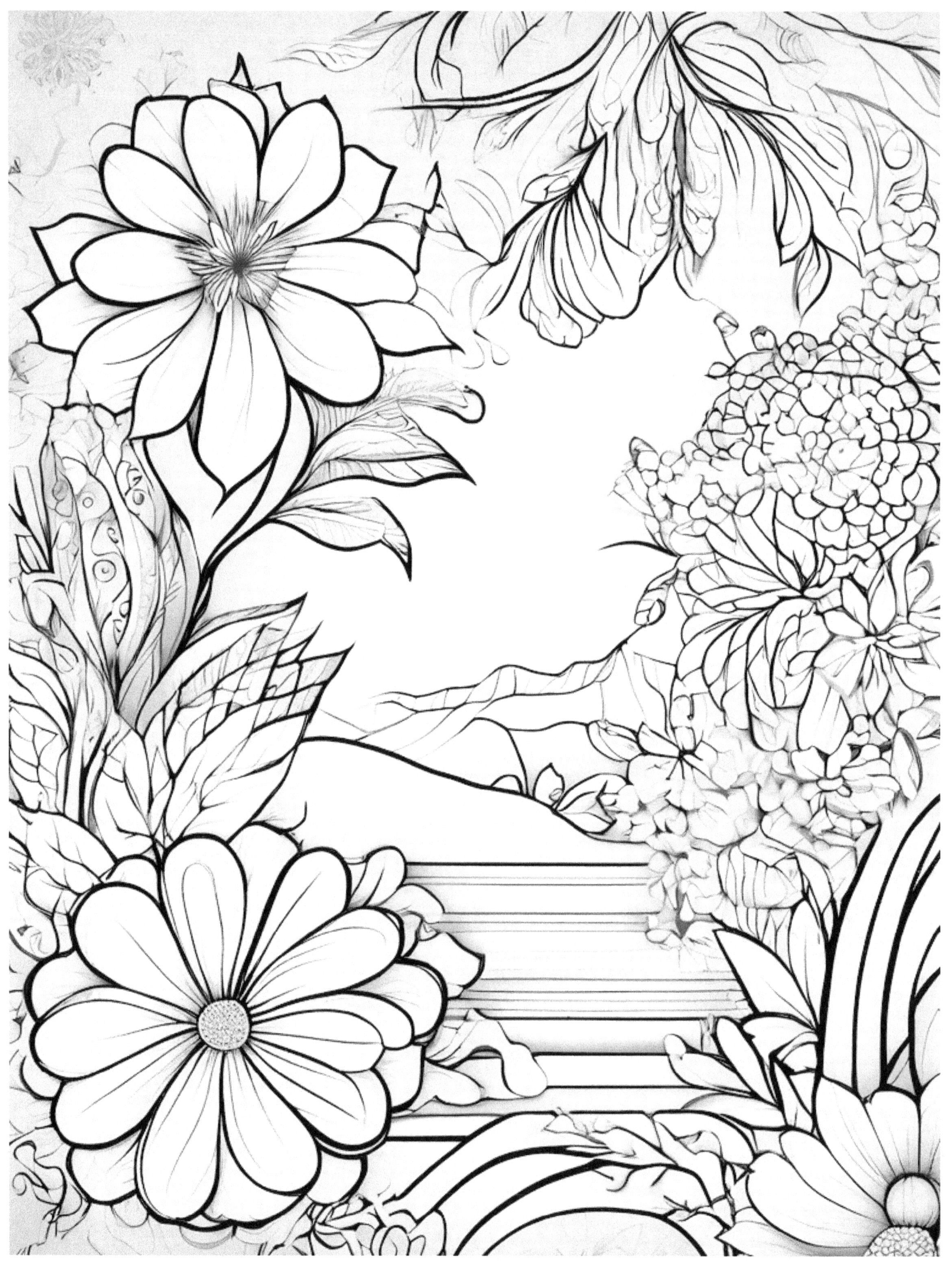

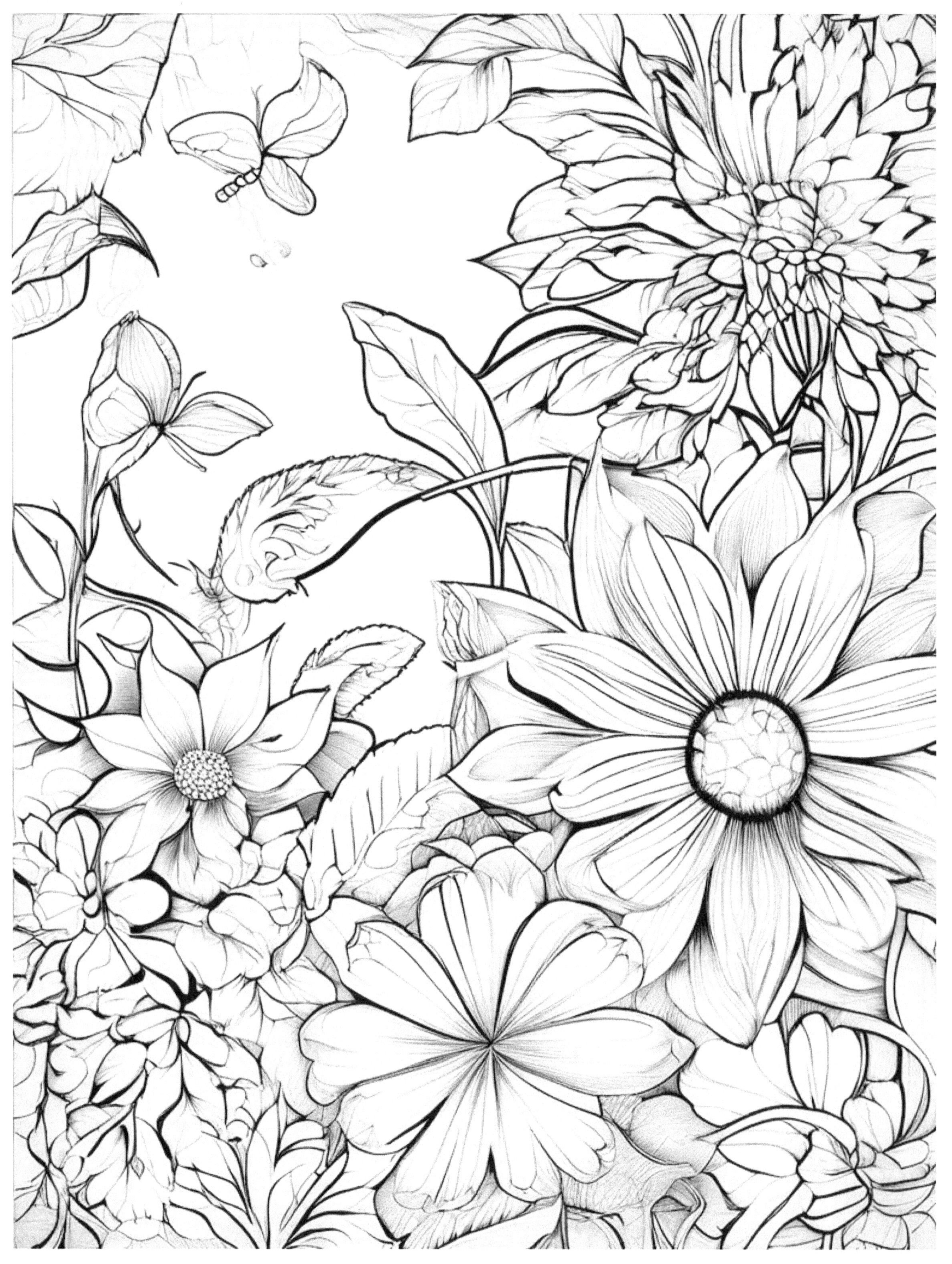

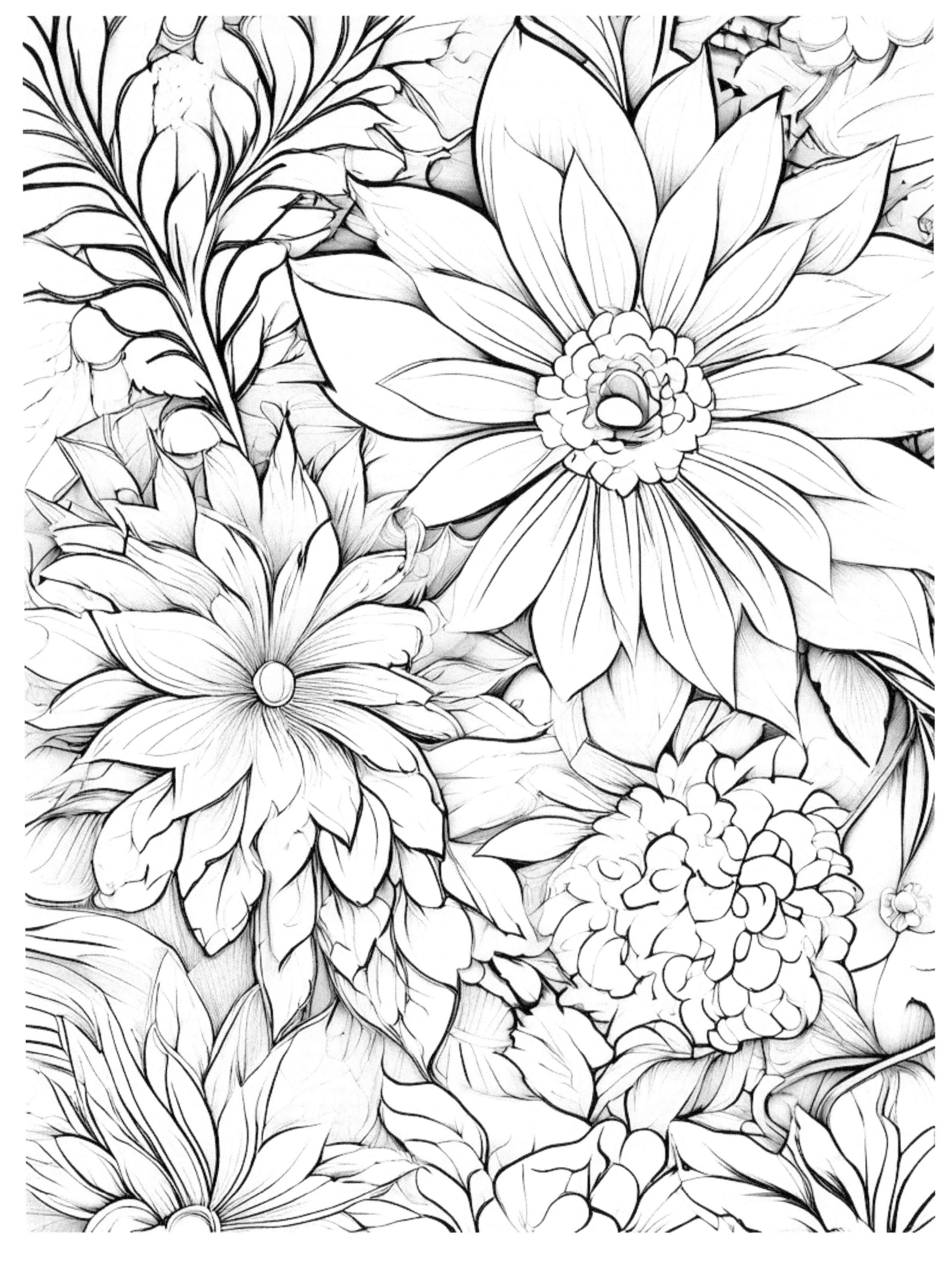

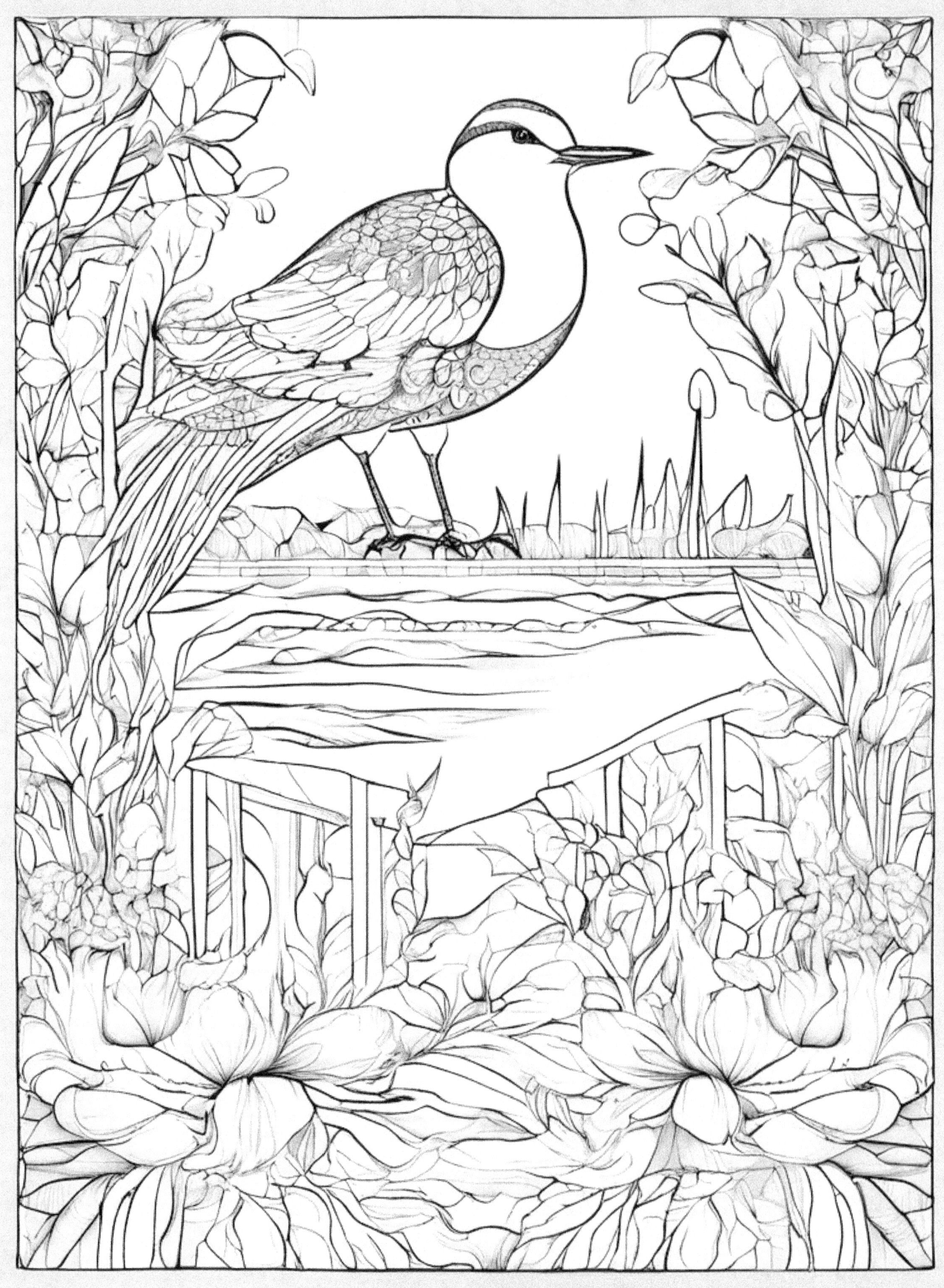

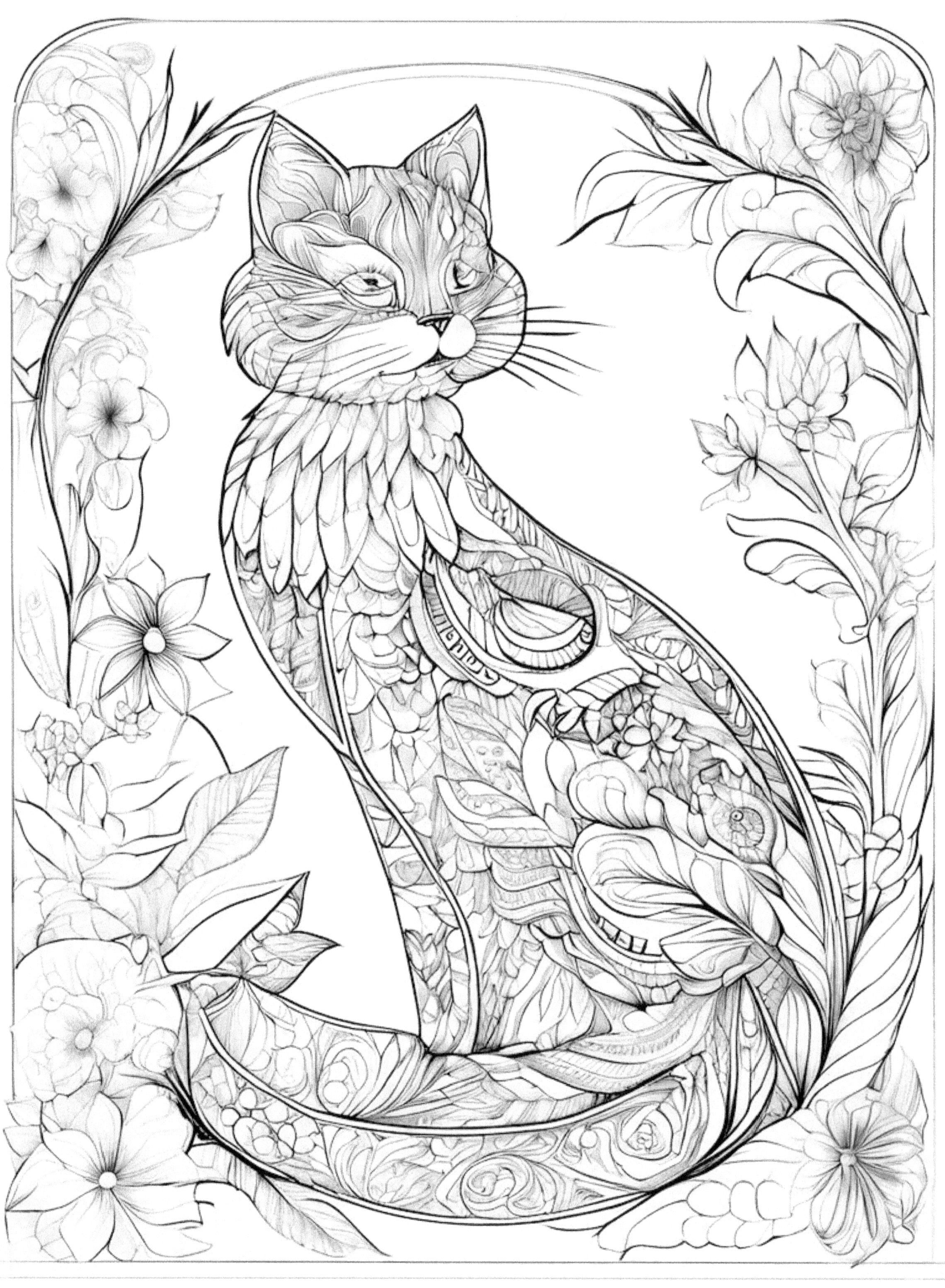

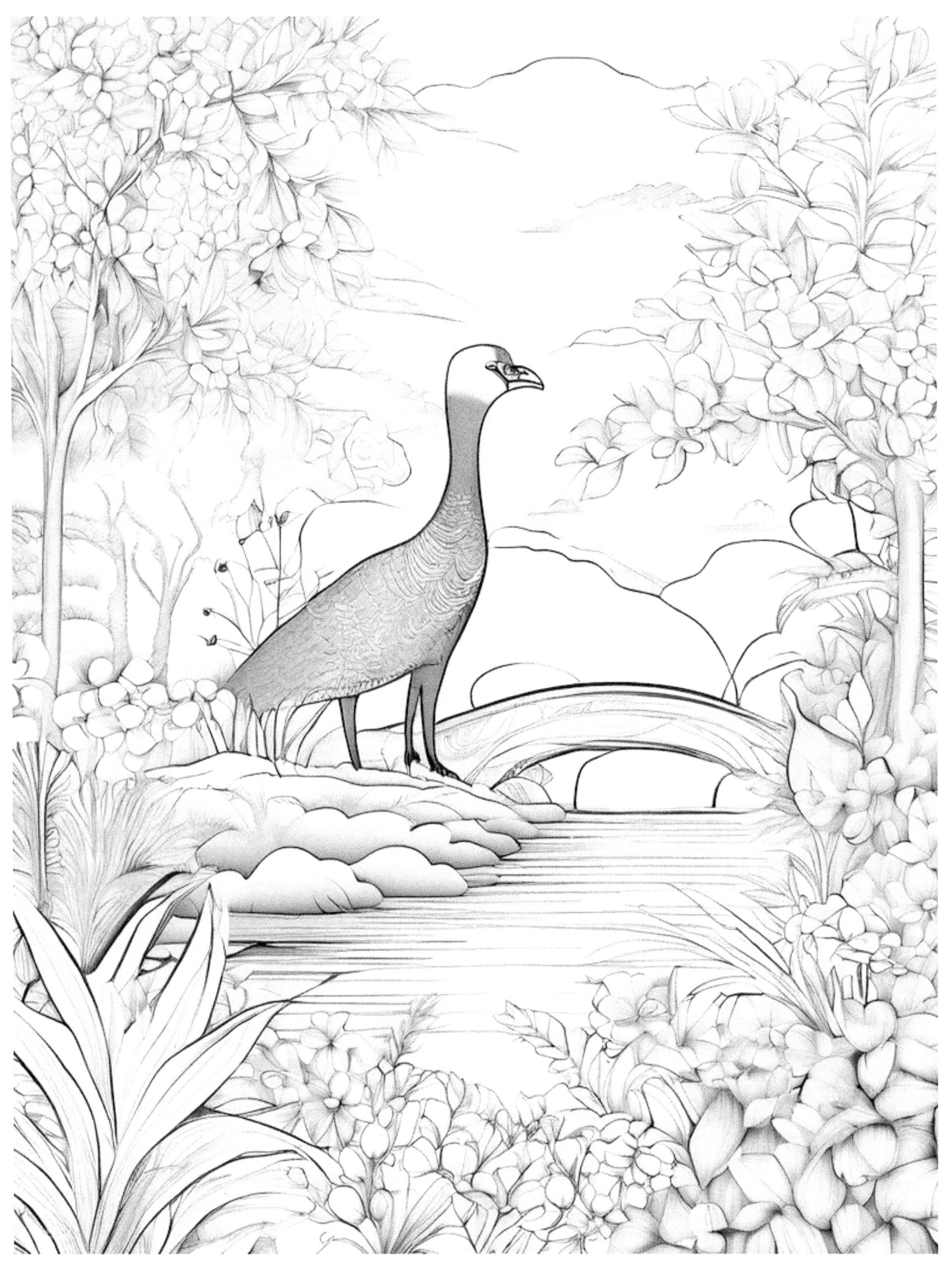

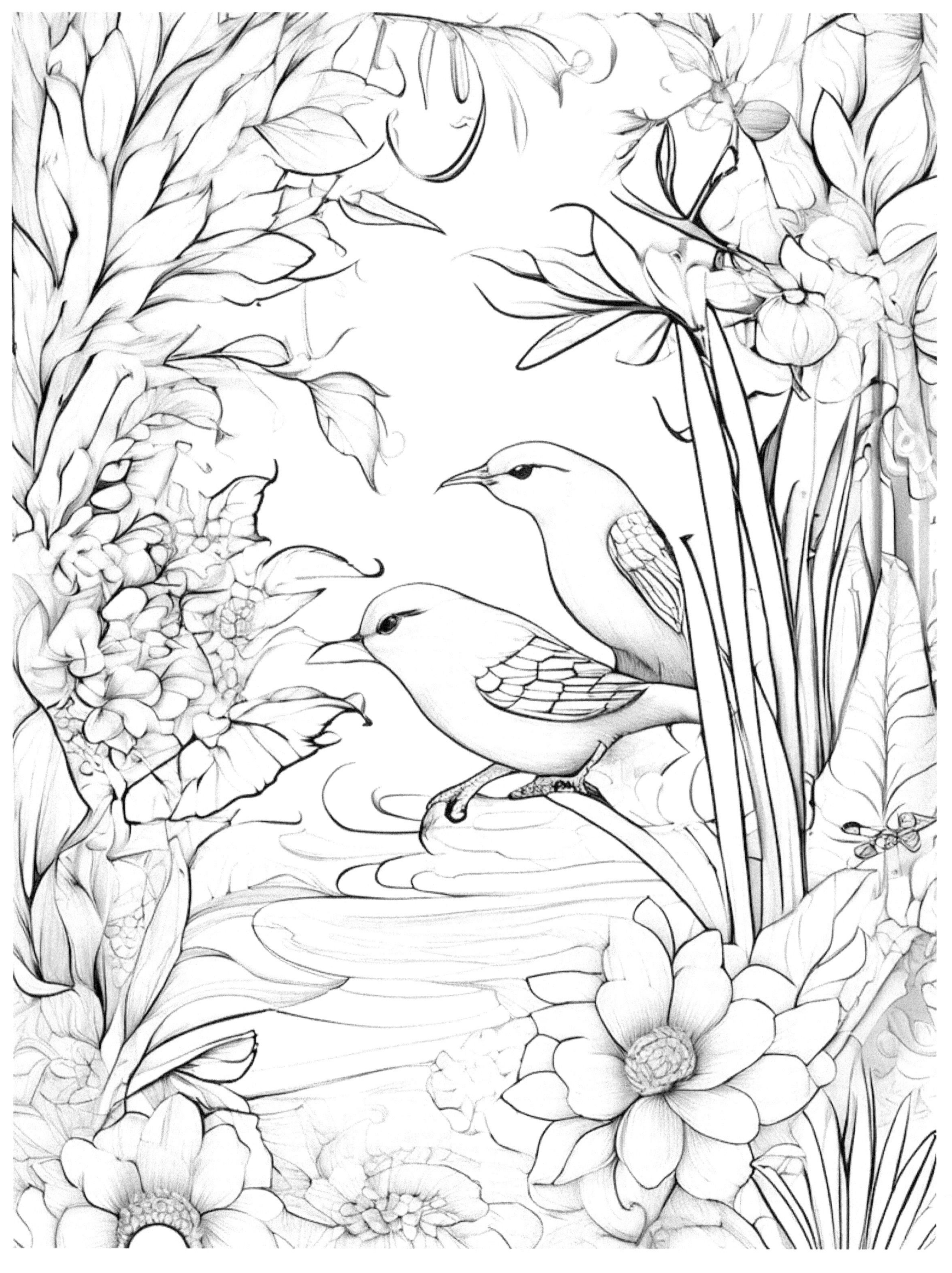

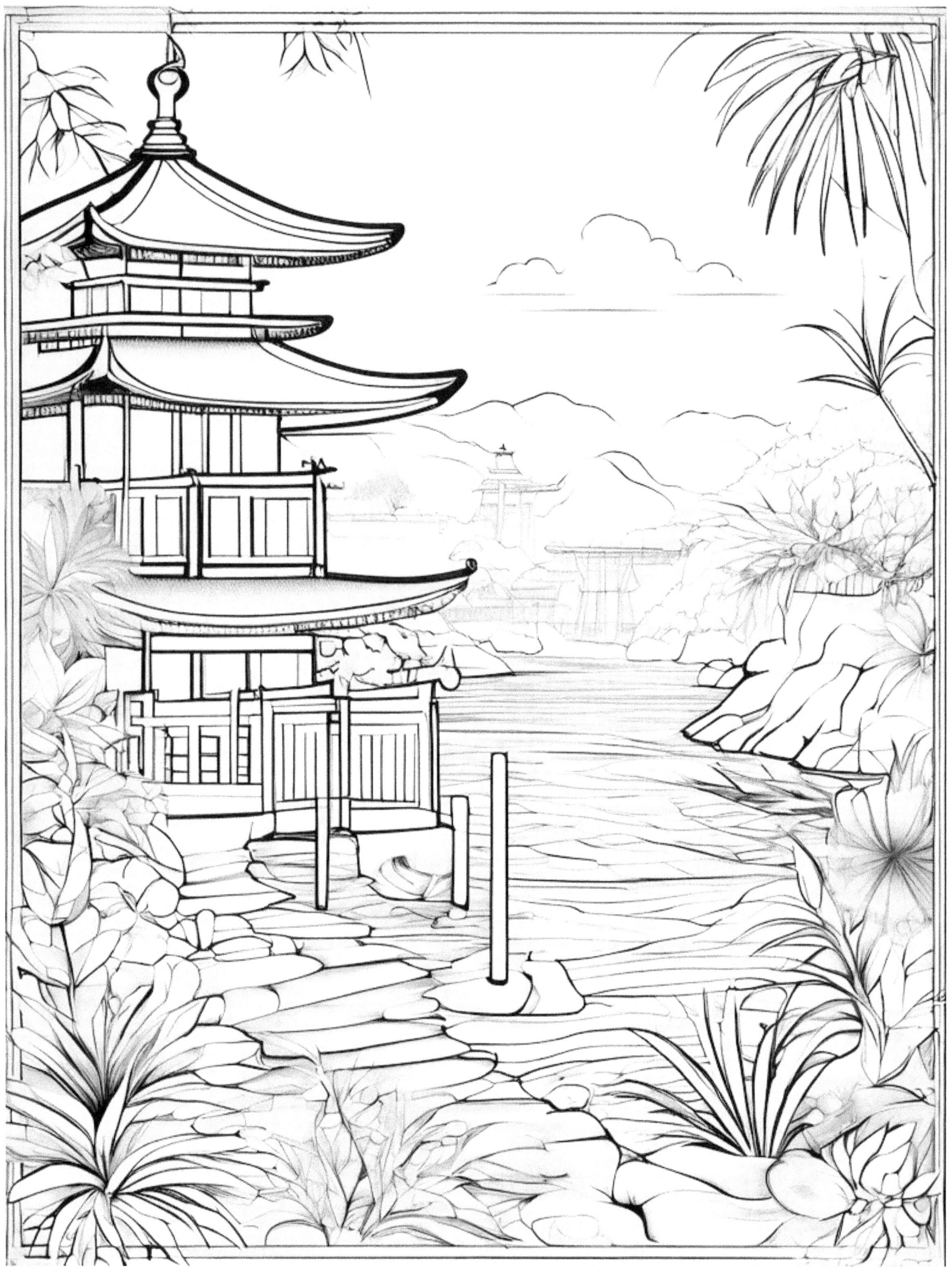

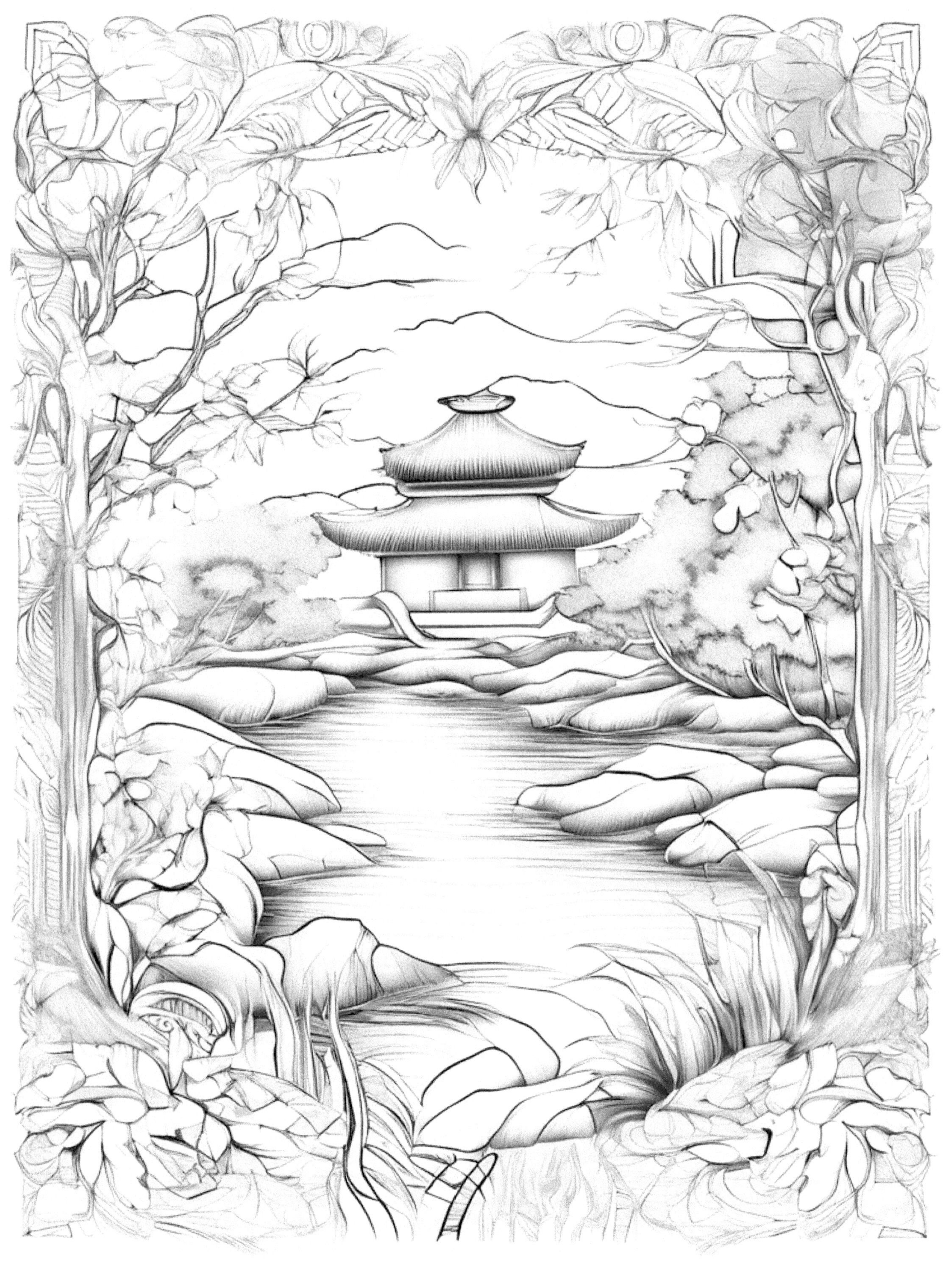

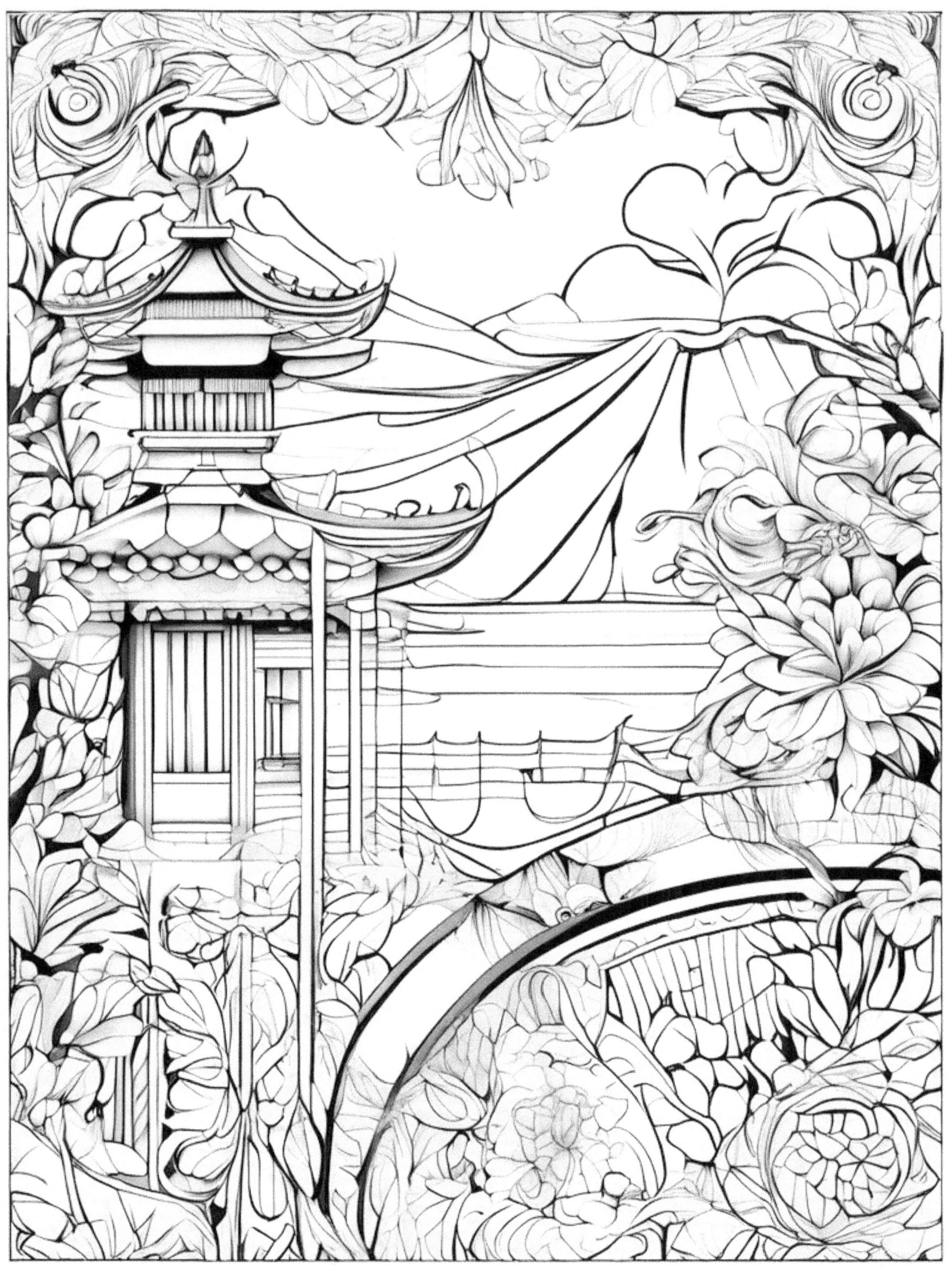

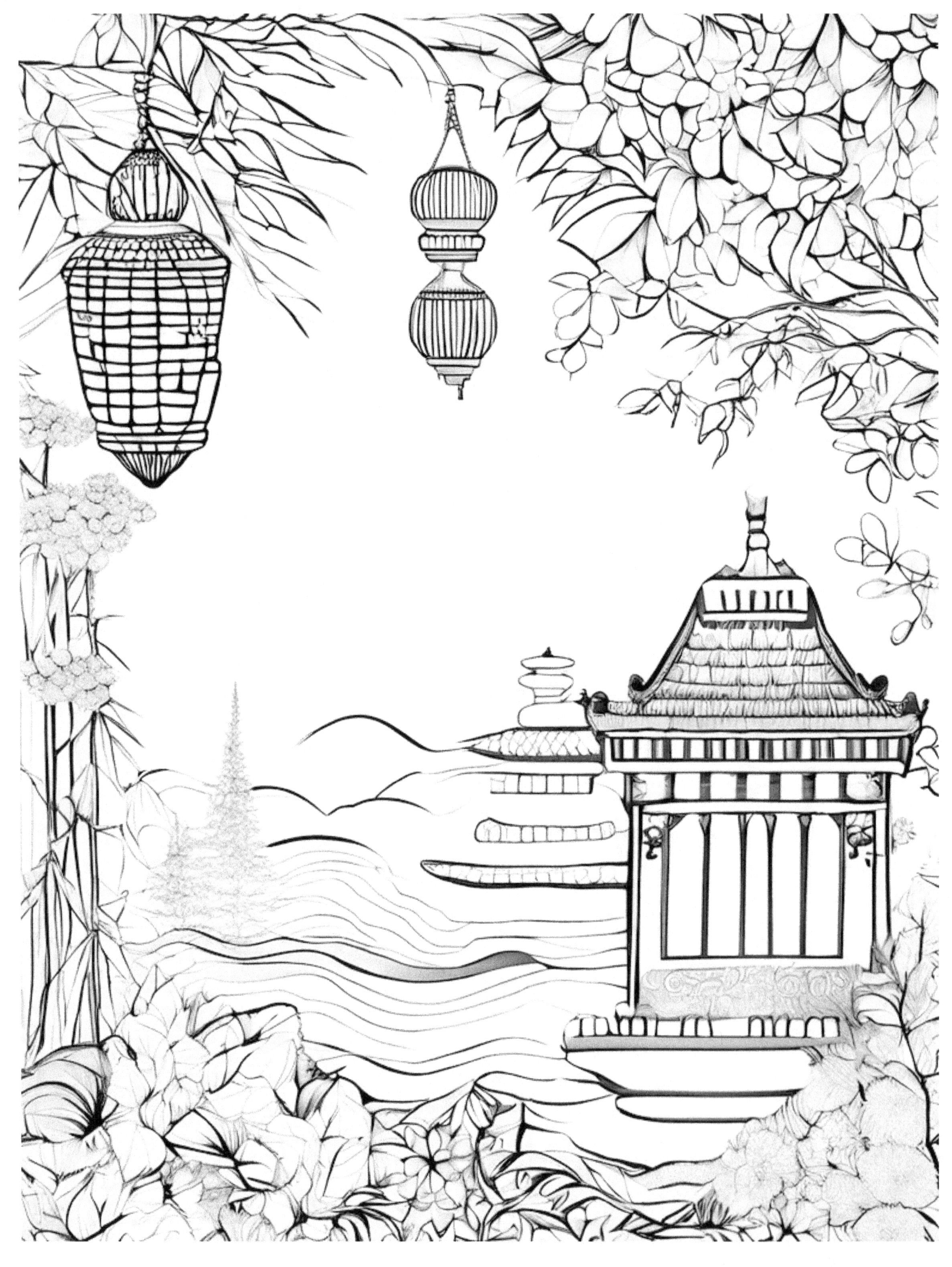

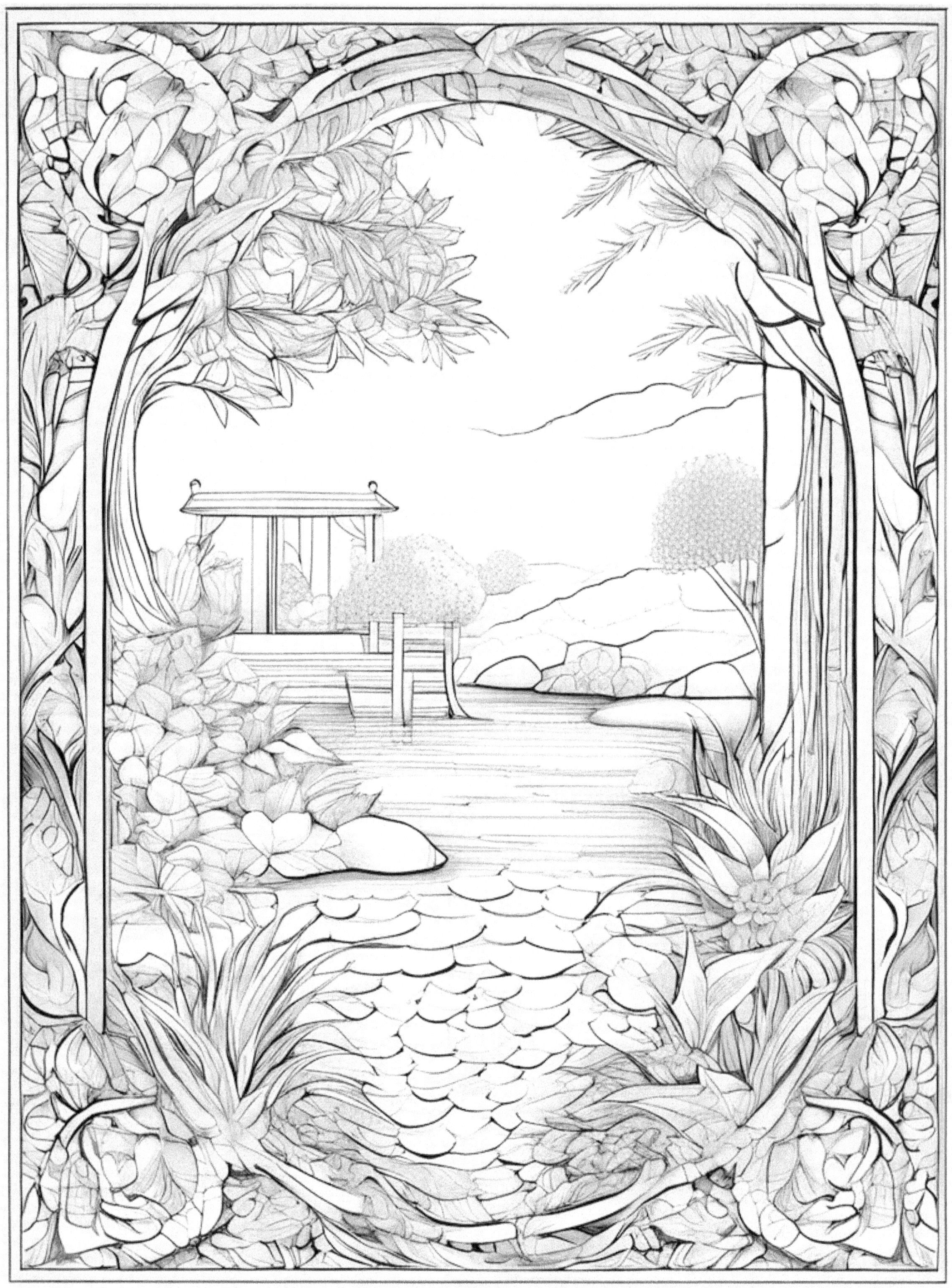

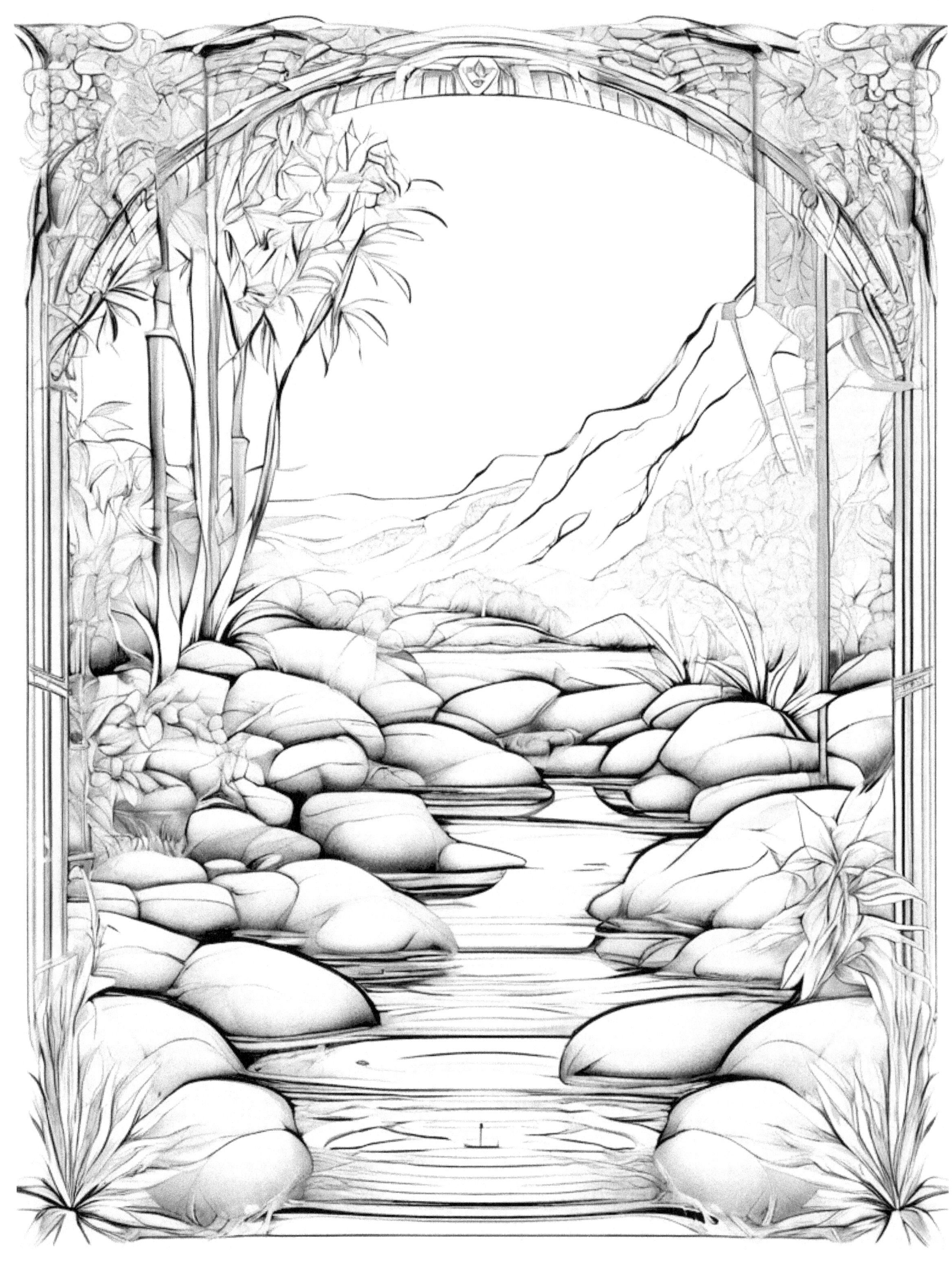

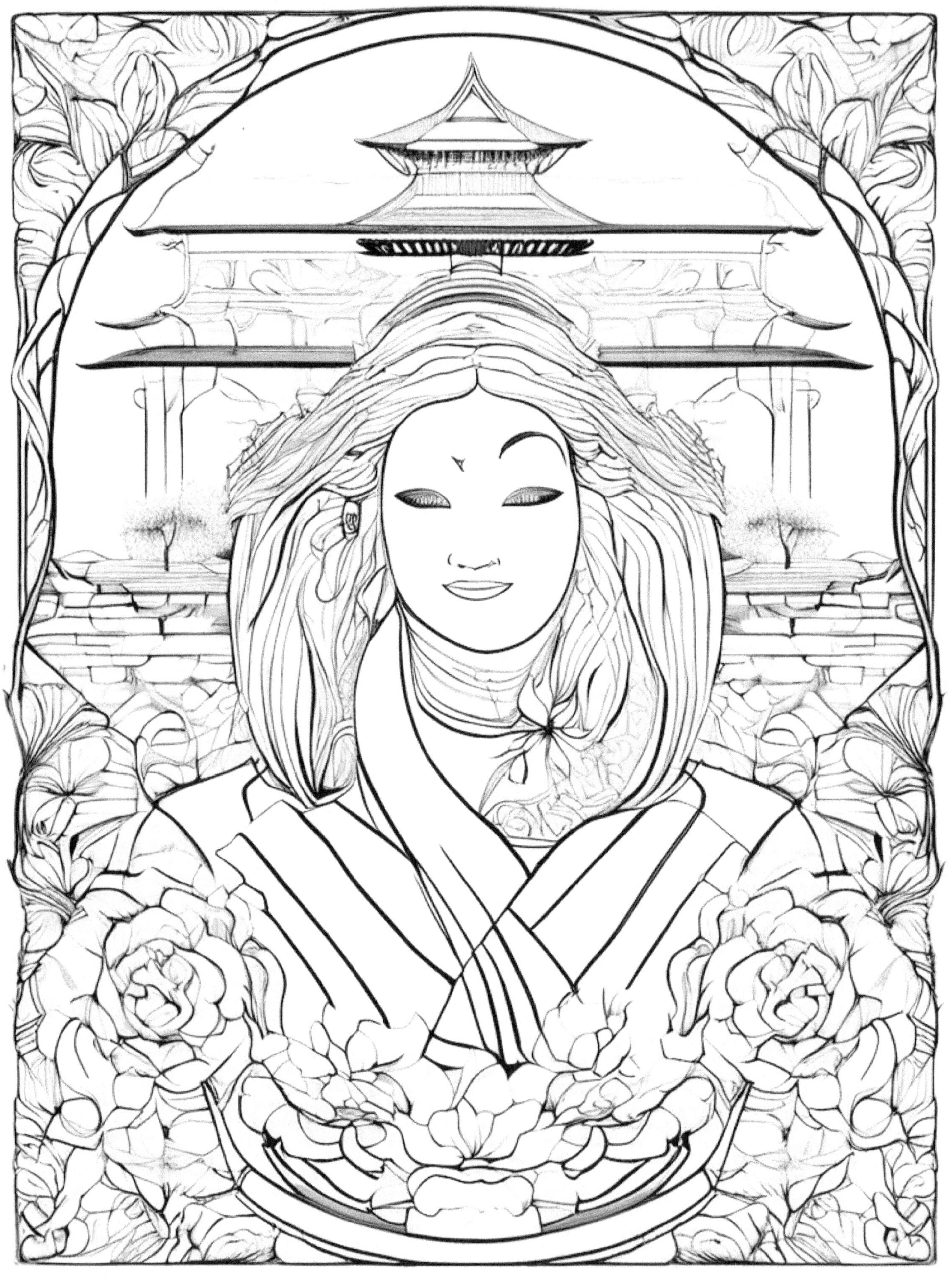

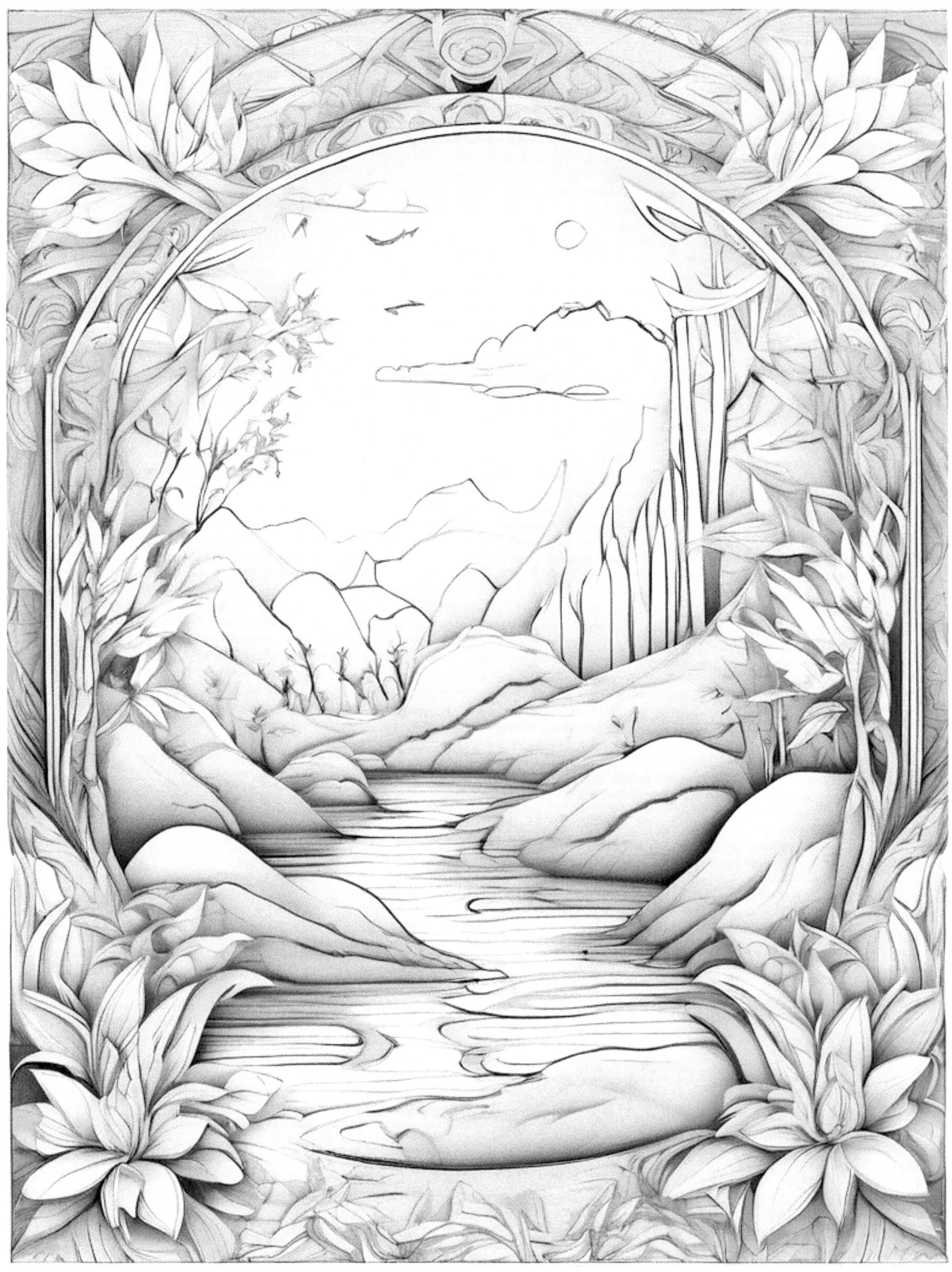

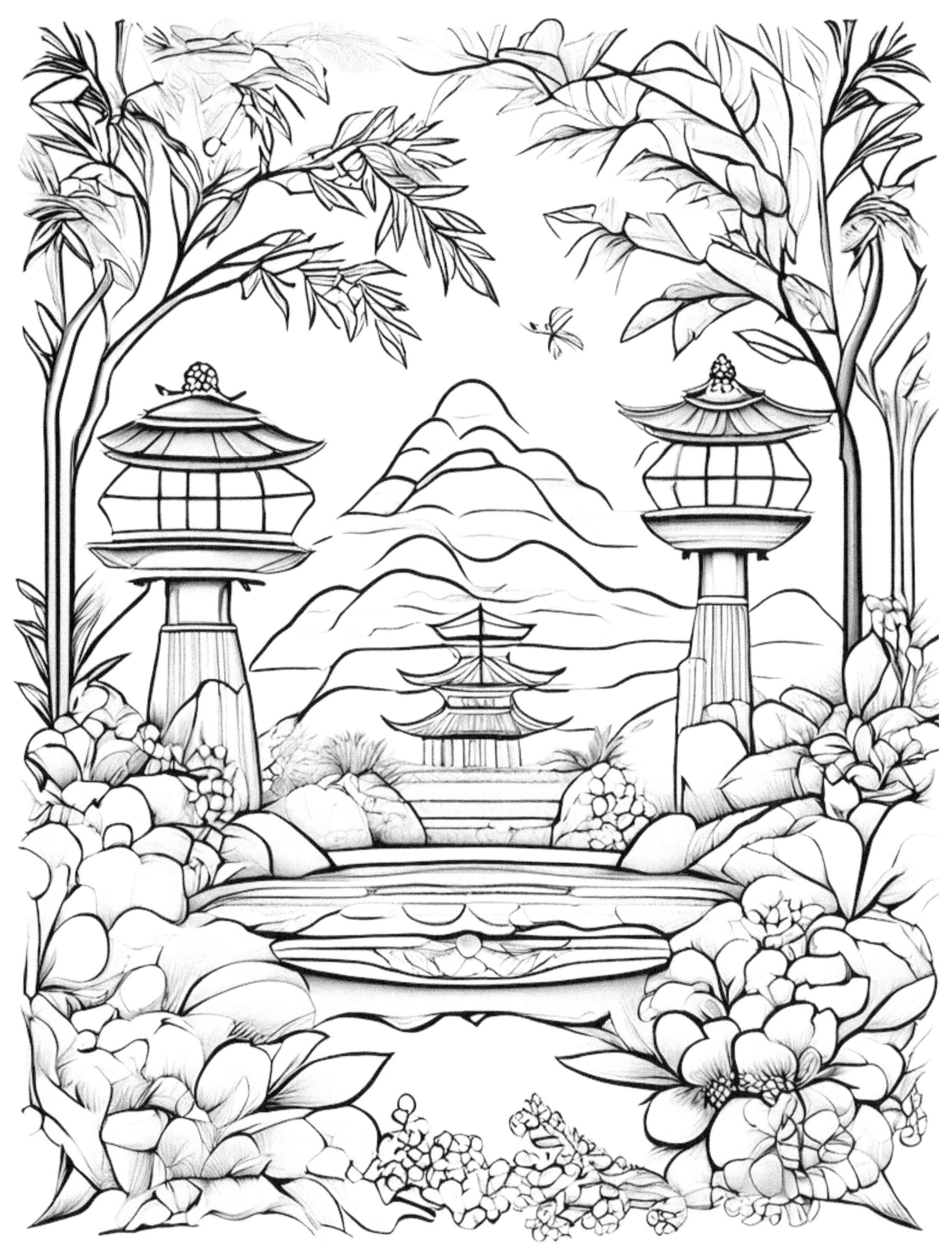

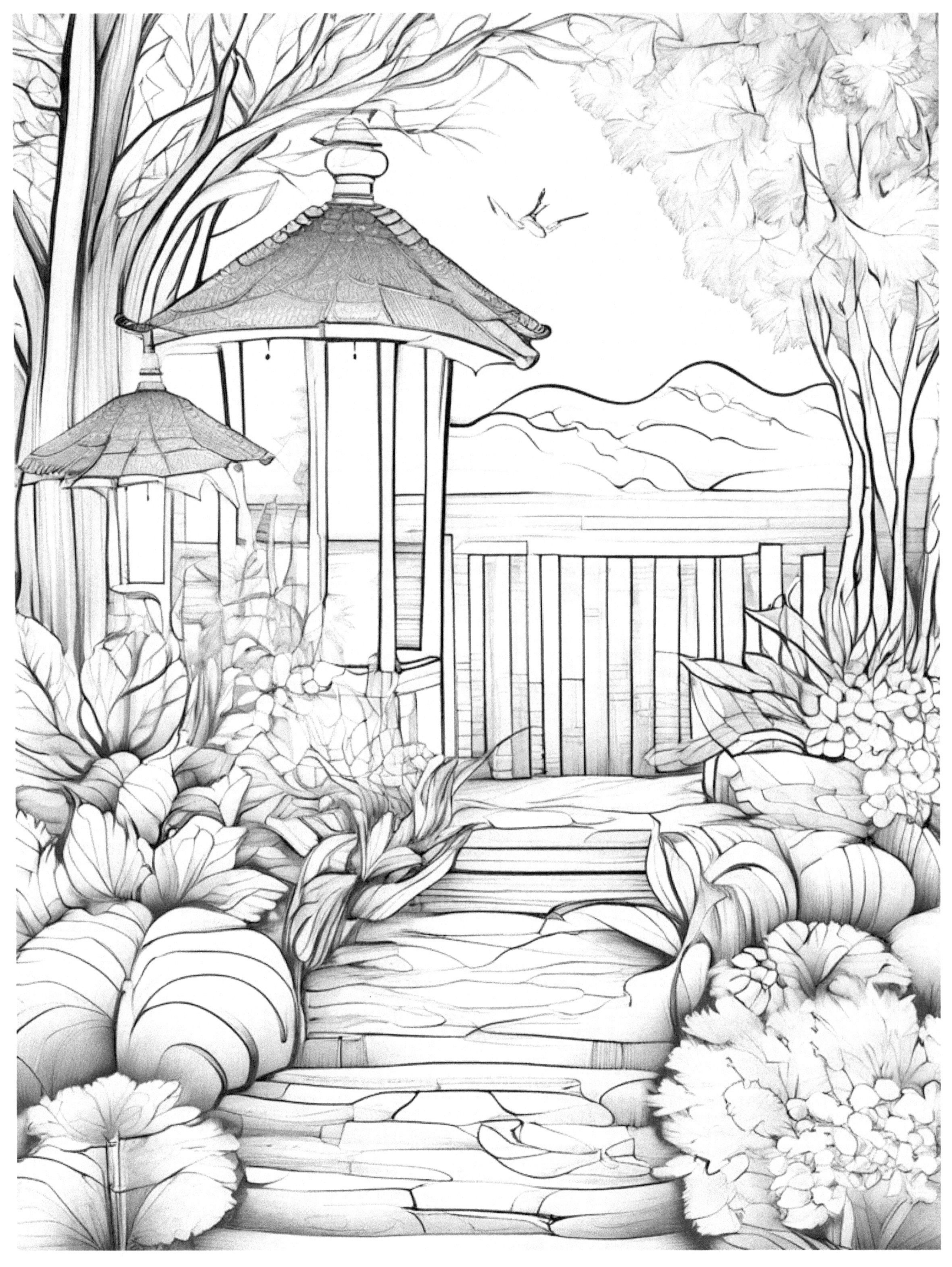

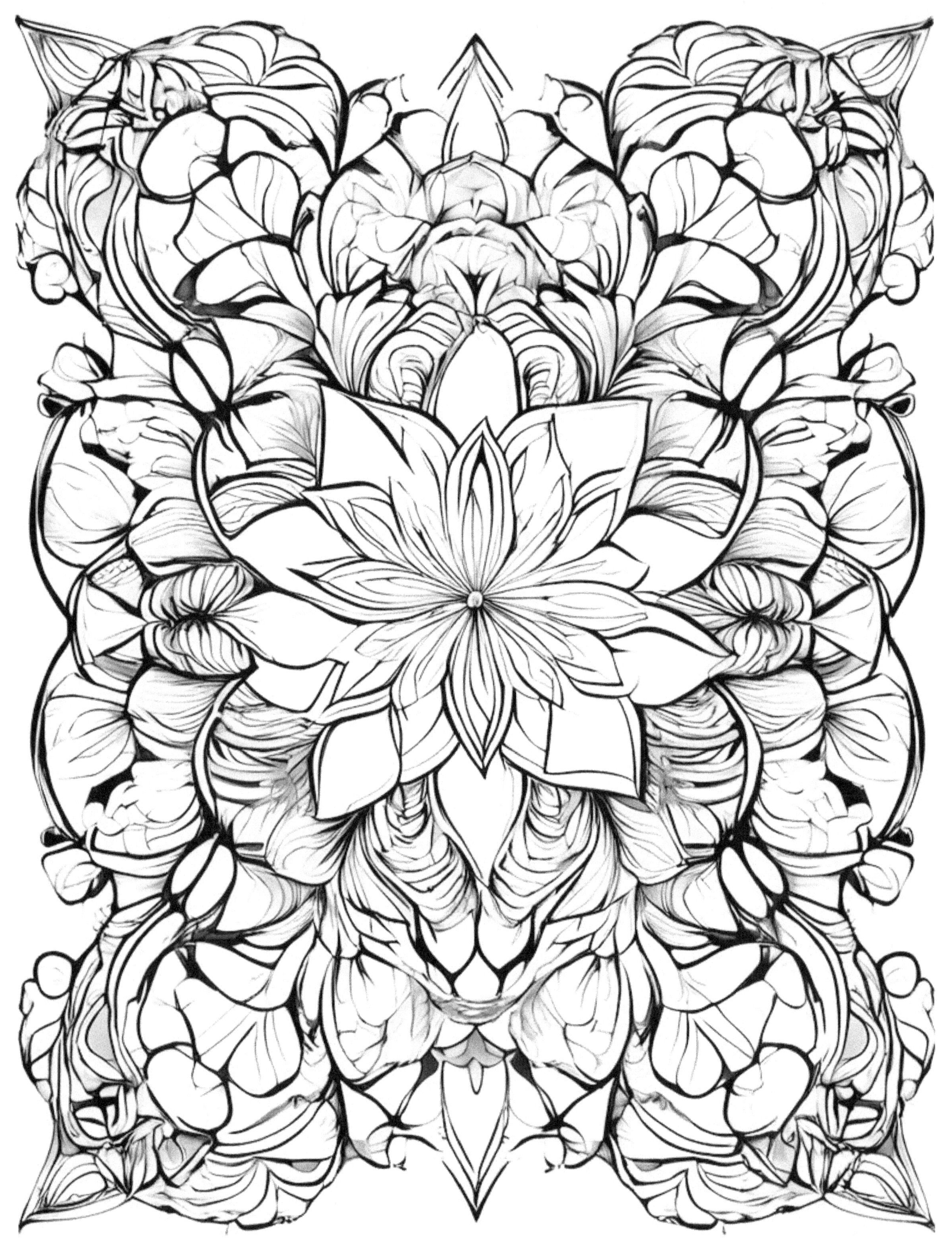

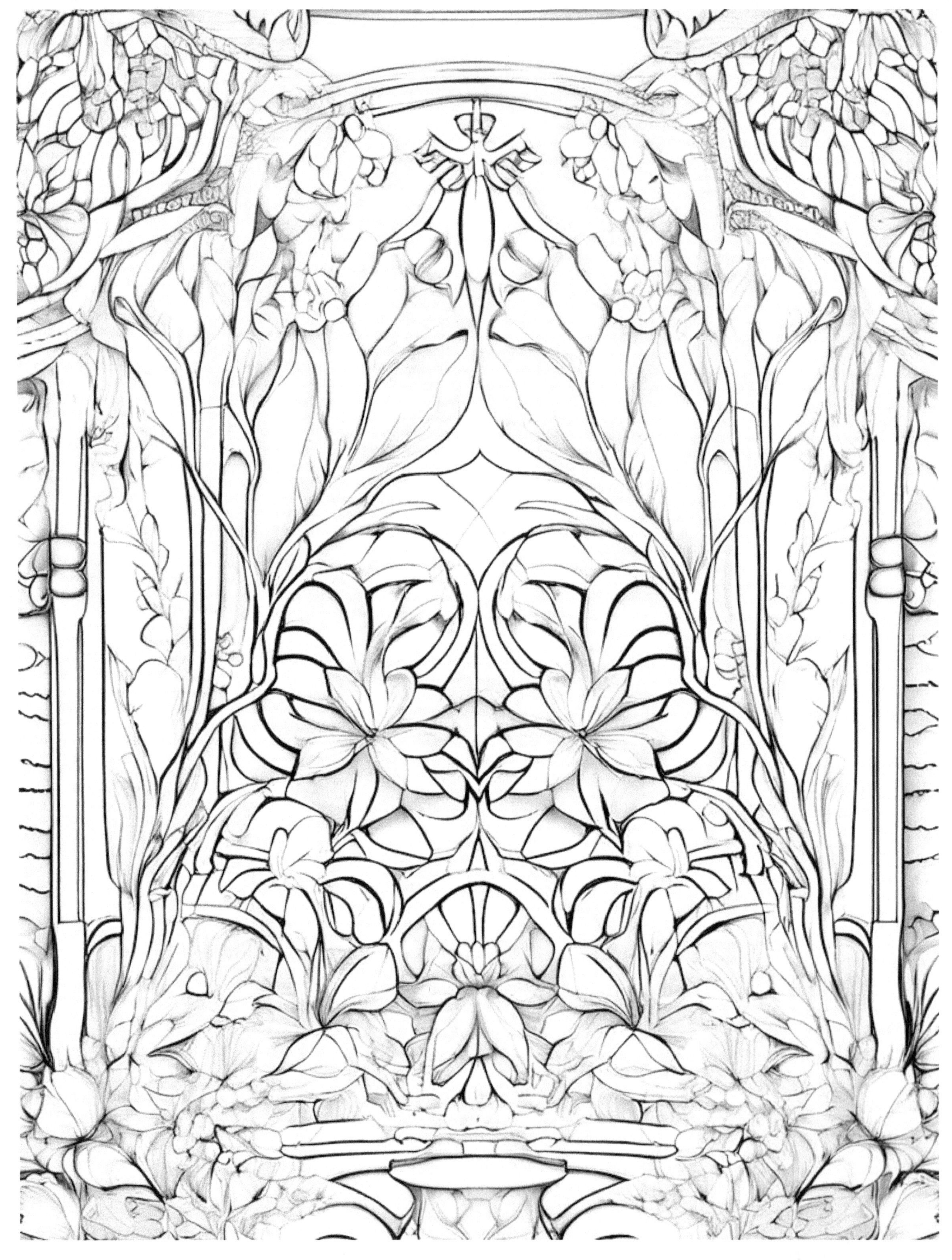

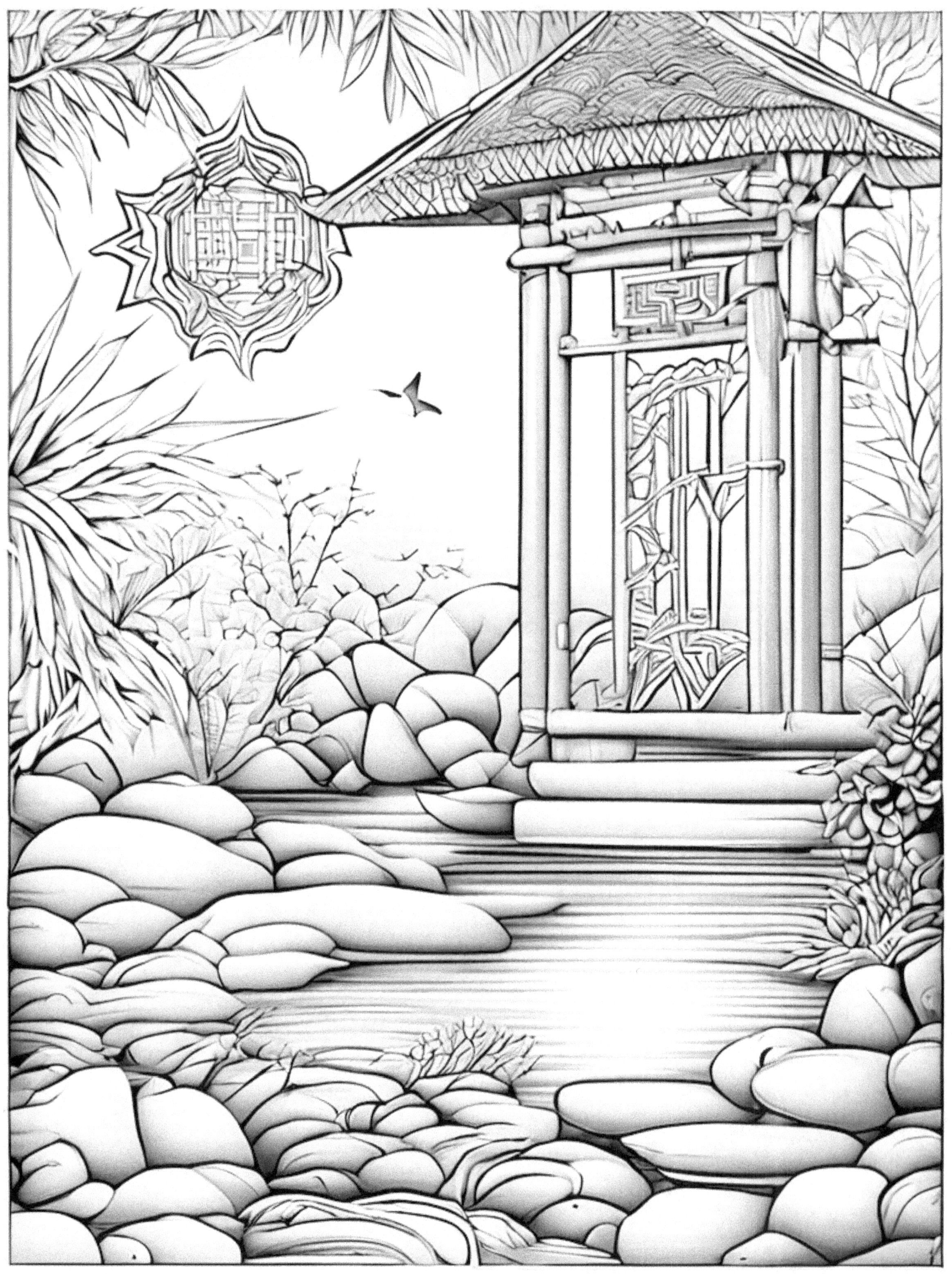

Remember, the pages that are now filled with your colors are a tangible representation of moments of peace and self-discovery.

May each work of art created be a reminder that harmony is at your fingertips, ready to be rediscovered whenever you need a refuge.

May the colors you bring to this book continue to light your path, bringing calm and joy to your life.

May the serenity you found here always remain with you, coloring not only the pages, but each day that unfolds in front of you.

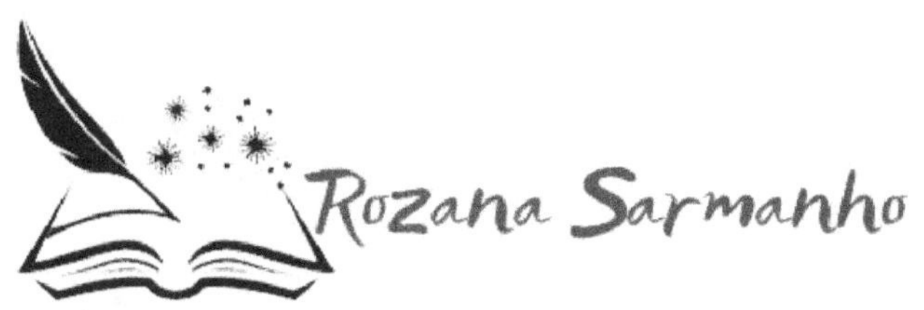